OFFICIALLY
WITHDRAWN

The Modern Wedding

From Graphics to Styling

GINGKO PRESS

The Modern Wedding
From Graphics to Styling

ISBN 978-1-58423-608-5

First Published in the United States of America by
Gingko Press by arrangement with
Sandu Publishing Co., Ltd.

Gingko Press, Inc.
1321 Fifth Street
Berkeley, CA 94710 USA
Tel: (510) 898 1195
Fax: (510) 898 1196
Email: books@gingkopress.com
www.gingkopress.com

Copyright © 2016 by Sandu Publishing
First published in 2016 by Sandu Publishing

Sponsored by Design 360°
– Concept and Design Magazine

Edited and produced by
Sandu Publishing Co., Ltd.

Book design, concepts & art direction by
Sandu Publishing Co., Ltd.
Chief Editor: Wang Shaoqiang
Design Director: Niu Huizhen

info@sandupublishing.com
www.sandupublishing.com

Printed and bound in China

• Contents •

Contents

Contents

Preface

Meghan Hopkins Sokorai: Owner/Founder of And Here We Are

A wedding invitation is the first chance a couple gets to set the tone of the event to come. Is it a formal, black-tie affair, or a casual barn party, or a hip rooftop bash? Once upon a time, wedding invitations looked mostly the same: a traditional calligraphic script centered, a sheet of tissue, a calligraphed envelope. Now we get to tell their stories with typography, illustration, color, and paper.

Modern wedding clients seek more personalized graphics for every step of their wedding, from the save-the-dates to invitations to menus, signage, programs and favors. These design-savvy couples want their invitations to speak to their personalities, their story, their wedding location, their pets, and even their favorite brunch spots. Our design approach is not much different from traditional branding; we create mood boards, overarching design concepts, iconography, type and color styles, and graphic elements such as monograms and illustrations, which function pretty much the same as a logomark.

In recent years there has been a renewed interest in hand-made graphics and tactile paper goods, and this is especially true in the wedding industry. Perhaps it's a pushback from our increasingly digital world, and maybe it's just the natural cycle of trends. Either way, the wedding invitation industry has been very influential in this revival of old practices, particularly hand lettering and analog printing processes. Our studio is able to keep the lights on – and I personally am able to be here writing this preface today – because of our custom wedding clients, who come to us requesting hand drawn lettering & illustrations, hand painted paper, letterpress printing, hot foil stamping, die cuts, and any other kind of custom hand-work we can envision.

As weddings and events become more personalized, a new class of creatives has cropped up to provide these services. Often, we have graphic design backgrounds, sometimes backgrounds in calligraphy or printing, and quite a few of us fell into this niche after designing our own weddings (myself included). We often work side by side with stylists and planners to create a cohesive event from top to bottom – no different than working on a branding project for a company. Working as a designer in the wedding industry, especially if you left the corporate world, is not without its challenges. Our clients can be inexperienced with the design process, and, they are understandably quite attached and emotionally involved with their project. If we're not careful to manage expectations, this can easily lead to an avalanche of emails, several concept redirections, and unexpected rounds of feedback and edits. It has taken years of experience to learn the delicate balance of the happiness of our clients with our own personal life. On the flip side, the significance of these events does influence us and truly makes the end result that much more gratifying. It's incredibly flattering to be invited to participate in such a large part of such an important day in a stranger's life – with some of those strangers becoming great friends along the way.

~~~~~~

About And Here We Are

And Here We Are is the design and letterpress printing studio of John and Meghan Sokorai, a husband and wife team who specialize in modern hand lettered and illustrated prints and stationery. Every piece is drawn, painted, and printed on antique letterpresses in their Columbus, OH studio.

"Invitations and save-the-dates set the tone of your overall event. The formality of your paper should match the formality of your wedding. This is the only chance you have to interact with your guests before the event itself, so the purpose is not only to inform, but also to excite."

Yonder Design

A Very Beloved Wedding

A destination wedding planning, design, and styling company available worldwide and based in Vienna, consisting of planners, designers, and artists with Elisabeth Cardich and Lorinda Horner at the heart of the team. The duo shares the same vision of creating moments with soul and events with a meaning. The team provides services including wedding design and styling, wedding planning, couple shoot production, floral design, and a rental collection of one-of-a-kind pieces for events for couples who want to get married anywhere on this planet.

Interview with
Elisabeth Cardich from A Very Beloved Wedding

When did you start your career as a wedding designer? Can you share with us the story behind it?
I have always been involved in the art and design industry in South America and Europe. Everything happened organically when friends and brides started to ask me for advice in terms of interior design and wedding design. Then I met my business partner, Lorinda Horner, who had her own wedding planning company. We decided to unite forces and found this company, merging professional project management with outstanding creative design.

How would you define AVBW's design style?
Our design is sparkling, timeless, original, honest, meaningful, happy, elegant, and cool. Sparkling because it surprises the viewer, timeless because you will always like it, original because we are innovators and creators, honest and meaningful because it is based on the love story of our couples, happy because life is all about enjoying it, elegant because as Coco Chanel said, "elegance is when the inside is as beautiful as the outside," and cool because it happens naturally. We take care to unite all these keywords that define us and make them substantial for our couples.

Toscana Nascosta is a very beautiful wedding. Can you share with us the story behind it?
Thank you, it was great teamwork with my partner Lorinda and the photographer! All of the work we do is meaningful;

that's why we say "we create moments with soul and events with a meaning." Toscana Nascosta is inspired by Goethe's Italian journey. Slipping away from duties, trying to discover yourself through the things you see, finding a meaning to words, learning to know yourself by and through objects of beauty, getting inspired, feeling free, happy and in love… unconditional love. Goethe was seeking paradise, just as we do, and he found it in Italy, just as we did.

In your opinion, what role do wedding graphics, including wedding stationery and decorations, play in a wedding?
They are essential! They are among others the key components of the wedding storyline, the leitmotif, and the design. With our design we put elements of look and feel together, creating an unforgettable experience for the couple, the guests, and the photographic and cinematic results. The graphics and stationery create an important glimpse of this experience.

For those who want to make their own wedding stationery and decorations, what suggestions would you give?
I would suggest to start with a wedding design concept and a mood board that at least has to take the aesthetics of the wedding into consideration. Upon that every decision you make as a couple is fine.

Olivia & Noah's Toscana Nascosta Wedding

*Wedding Design
and Planning:
A Very Beloved
Wedding*

*Photography:
Melanie Nedelko*

*Dress:
Victoria Ruesche*

*Stationery
Design:
Milia Ink*

*Floral Design:
A Very Beloved
Bloom*

*Venue:
Villa Sermolli*

*Elisabeth's
Photo:
Tony Gigov*

The color palette included lemon yellow, olive green, off-white and beige and gold accents; the atmosphere and experience were Mediterranean.

The design and styling were all about lemons and olive trees, spring and summer, white sculptures and forbidden gardens.

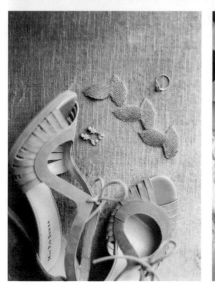

Wedding designer Elisabeth Cardich wrote a poem inspired by Tuscany.

Spring under my feet.
Summer in my heart.
It is because of you, I can feel
the perfumes of blossoming
spring flowers.
Because of you I love the fresh
lemons in my mouth.
Because of you I see white
sculptures in forbidden
gardens.
Because of you I feel this
moment.

The materials were organic, woody, and silky, the stationery was soft and natural, the flowers fresh and free and the couple elegant and in love.

Joel Serrato

Life and happenstance led Joel to become a filmmaker and photographer who infuses his love of movement in capturing moments of innocence, laughter, love, and life. He has carved out a niche in the filmmaking world as the reigning king of Super 8 weddings, taking the art of storytelling to a whole new level. His films are pure emotion wrapped in the artistic coupling of nostalgic moments with intimate takes on real life.

Interview with
Joel Serrato, Photographer

When did you start your career as a wedding photographer? Can you share with us the story behind it?

I've been photographing weddings for almost 2 years now. My background in the wedding industry started as a filmmaker, for almost 8 years I've filmed weddings and events for my clients. Photography stemmed from my clients asking me to photograph and film their families after their wedding. Naturally, I fell in love with the still life of photographs and try my best to incorporate motion from filmmaking into stills. It's even more challenging to freeze a moment in time, and I'm in love with the challenge!

How would you define your photography style?

I wouldn't say I have a specific style; every wedding is different and has its beauty and challenges. I'd say my style is very adaptive to people, love, and the fast moving dynamic of a wedding day.

Hayley & Dave's Wedding is a very beautiful project. Can you share with us the story behind it?

Laurie Arons of Laurie Arons Special Events, who is a dominating force in the wedding design and production world introduced me to Hayley, a production manager for her company. I instantly fell in love with her! Hayley and Dave are probably the happiest clients I've ever had. They are so gracious and kind, which made me work harder for them – I really thrive on people's energy, and Hayley and Dave's wedding was surrounded with love from my vendor friends in the industry. We were all just running around doing what we always do, while wiping a tear here and there with excitement from one of our own getting married!

In your opinion, what role do wedding stationery and decorations play in a wedding?

Wedding stationery and design elements play a crucial role in weddings. Couples take this time to design and interpret their lives and likes to welcome their guests and showcase their love on such a special day. I'm just the lucky one who gets to photograph all the pretty things that come along with that special day.

Event Design:
Laurie Arons
Special Events

Photography:
Joel Serrato

Stationery
Design:
Pitbulls And
Posies

Floral Design:
Kathleen Deery
Design

Printed Marerials:
Amber Moon
Design

Calligraphy:
Curlicue Designs

THE PLEASURE OF YOUR COMPANY
IS REQUESTED AT THE MARRIAGE OF

Hayley
Robin Crombie

&

Davi
James K

TENTH OF OCTO
IN THE AFTER

IN THE GARDEN
ASE L
Y, CA NIA

OR FOLLOW

SEASIDE CHIC

Map of Memories

CAVALLO
POINT
where we
fell in love

THE COZY
AT NOE
first apartment

THE
BOATHOUSE
first house

EUPEC
KASTILLE
where we toast
with French 75s

CSS
first kiss

Map Illustrations by Joanie Cro

Set Sail F
#thedayle

RSVP
Please reply
by September 18th to
thedayley@gmail.com

" When you realize you want
to spend the rest of your life
with somebody , you want
the rest of your life
to start as soon as possible "

Hayley and Dave's family-oriented ceremony was held on the beach in Half Moon Bay. The couple wanted the special day to be focused on fun, love, and happiness, and the team created the right atmosphere for them through every detail including the papers, florals, and decorations.

The couple had their reception in the groom's parents' backyard to make it intimate and special for their family and closest friends. The seaside setting was decorated with the groom's favorite color: orange.

Lovely custom details were found everywhere, from the Capiz wind chime escort display featuring Samantha Singson-Martin's calligraphy to fun lucite cocktail menus by Amber Moon Design.

Yonder Design

Generally involved at the early stages of an event, the team specializes in conceptualizing and designing save-the-dates, websites, and invitations, assisting event planners in executing and developing their ideas to create cohesive and well branded events. Their initial graphic designs, which lay the framework of elements that will be carried through to the actual event itself, are all done in their San Francisco-based studio.

Interview with
Chris Neubauer from Yonder Design

When did you start your career as a wedding invitation designer?
Yonder was founded by my wife Julie and I in the early part of 2013. My background was in magazine publishing and Julie's was in graphic design and painting. Paper and ink was very familiar to both of us, but in different, yet complementary ways.

How would you define Yonder's design style?
Our style varies quite dramatically from client to client based on their tastes, but an overarching aesthetic trend we strive for is a sense of refined simplicity. We love incorporating textures, materials, and techniques that aren't ordinarily used in print design.

Michelle & Emma's Coastal Wood Suite is delicate and stylish. What was your inspiration?
The backdrop for this event was a stunning private estate along the cliffs in Big Sur, California. We wanted to bring the natural elements of the area into the designs, while keeping true to the couple's clean and modern aesthetic.

Seagrass, wood, tumbled glass, and paper were combined in subtle ways so as not to overpower the natural beauty of the venue.

In your opinion, what role do wedding invitations and save-the-date cards play in a wedding?
Invitations and save-the-dates set the tone of your overall event. The formality of your paper should match the formality of your wedding. This is the only chance you have to interact with your guests before the event itself, so the purpose is not only to inform, but also to excite. A well branded and cohesive paper suite gives an event a continuity that many lack.

For those who want to craft their own wedding stationery and decorations, what suggestions would you give?
Creating a plan from the beginning is very important to create a sense of cohesiveness. Try to be consistent in the paper being used and printing technique on each of your pieces. Pay close attention to paper weights because people often overlook how something feels in guests' hands.

Design:
Yonder Design

Photography:
Sasha Gulish

Event Design:
Shannon Leahy
Events

Floral Design:
Atelier Joya

An open-air tent was designed to capture the refreshing sea breeze and the sound of the waves crashing below. Yonder created the wedding suite with a custom starfinder for the location and date, custom painted signage, letterpress printed programs with wood veneer and the couple's monogram, and handkerchiefs for happy tears. Pashminas (in case guests got chilly) and welcome baskets for guests were also prepared.

Green and white florals
were housed within clear
glass and cement vessels,
along with votives
wrapped in natural
seagrass.

Escort cards weighted down with seaglass, geometric menus, and custom glazed tile table numbers were used together to create a romantic and elegant atmosphere.

Park & Grove

A Los Angeles-based full service event design and production studio created in 2013 by Sarah Tolboe and Marla Weintraub with a combined 14+ years experience in the event industry. They share an overwhelming passion for events and a meticulous eye for design more than anything.

Interview with
Marla Weintraub from Park & Grove

When did you start your career as a wedding event designer? What's the story behind it?
I fell into events while I was in college, which ultimately led to my first internship with a wedding planner and I've been doing them ever since. I had the opportunity to work for some of the greatest planners in the industry, which ultimately led to starting Park & Grove with my business partner, Sarah. Sarah's creativity and my logistical sense made for the perfect partnership when it comes to designing and producing events.

How would you define Park & Grove's design style?
Understated elegance. We believe that it's best to focus on the simple, special details and creating something truly personal.

The project showcased here was your own wedding – what was your inspiration for this design?
Our home has always had a very neutral palette (we share a general aversion to bright color), so our wedding coloration consisted of shades of gray, beige, taupe, and gold accents. Our wedding was loosely Italian inspired as Casa Elar is a Tuscan inspired estate and we wanted to reflect that in our overall design (dark wood, aged stone, etc.).

In your opinion, what role does paper play in a wedding?
Paper is one of the design elements in a wedding where you can showcase some real creativity. Our paper designer created a custom crest with our initials that we introduced in our save-the-date and carried through to our wedding day. From beginning to end it was one continuous story that really fit our overall aesthetic and personalities.

For those who want to do their own wedding stationery and decorations, what suggestions would you give?
Keep it simple! We come from a philosophy that less is more and the most important thing is taking a single design concept and doing it well, as opposed to incorporating every option you come across.

What do you think of our book?
What a beautiful way to feature so many different weddings and a wide array of designs and personalities. It serves as a reminder that this wonderful industry is so diverse and designers are creating stunning weddings all over world that are truly reflective of the couples being celebrated.

*Event Design:
Park & Grove
Event Studio*

*Photography: Joel
Serrato*

*Stationery
Design:
BB Paper & Ink*

*Floral Design:
Kelly Kaufman
Design*

Marla and Andrew's wedding was held at Casa Elar, a Tuscan inspired estate in Ojai, California. Keeping true to its surroundings, the wedding infused natural elements into a timeless and classic design with simple, yet elegant custom details.

Both Andrew and Marla share a general aversion to overly bright colors, so the more muted palette consisting of shades of gray, beige, cream, and taupe with gold accents was fitting for the couple.

Estelle David

Estelle and Adam contemplated whether they should do a destination wedding by the beach and came across Moby Dicks, which incorporated everything they wanted in one. It had the beach, seemed enough removed to feel like a getaway, and was surrounded by beautiful trees and landscape. When they went to view the venue it was like love at first sight – that view over the beach and the cottage décor are to die for.

Interview with
Estelle David, Bride

What is your wedding theme? How did you come up with it?

My inspiration for the theme was to have the look and feel of a rustic romantic bush fairytale. After pinning all images I loved on Pinterest, my stylist and I really put together the exact look and feel that I had imagined.

What was your favorite part of the special day?

The whole day was a memory to never forget. To narrow it down to one is just simply too hard, but one of my favorites would be seeing Adam for the first time down the end of the isle. The suspense you go through the whole day until that moment when you see all the guests and your husband-to-be, it was the most overwhelming thing I have ever felt. The second favorite memory would be seeing my 85-year-old Nanna dancing with the family at the end of the night. She was so cute!

In your opinion, what role do the wedding suite and decoration play in a wedding?

Wedding styling and the special touches really create a way to make the atmosphere and vibe at a wedding.

For those who want to "DIY" their wedding suite and decorations, what suggestions would you give?

Leave plenty of time to DIY your wedding as the day comes around so fast and you don't want to stress trying to get things done by the big day. Get family and friends to help out to share the workload; this also makes more people feel involved on the big day and they feel grateful to be able to help.

*Stationery
Design:
Minted*

*Photography:
Lara Hotz
Photography*

*Event Design:
Piccolo & Poppi*

The bride was especially fond of the his and hers vows books, which featured elegant calligraphy and illustrations on the covers.

The arch surrounding the bridal table, with the beach as its backdrop, was a special detail of the day. The bride had imagined the scene to look as if they were sitting in the bush surrounded by candles and golden goodness, and that was exactly the effect created.

Her flower girl held a giant balloon with "here comes the bride" written on it – it was used just before the bride walked down the aisle, and looked great in photos. As the wedding wasn't held in a church or other venue with doors, a welcome sign helped designate an entrance in the beach-side park for guests when they arrived.

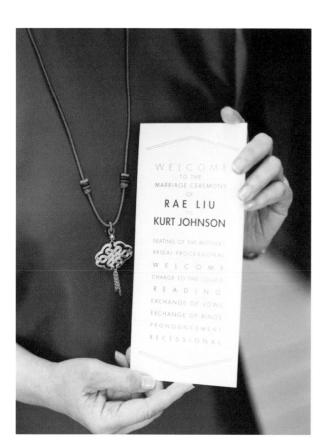

Rae & Kurt's Modern Suite

Design: Southern Fried Paper
Photography: Sarah Kate

The couple's overall style was very clean, minimal, and modern, but the bride also loved lush and overgrown florals featuring unique blooms and textures. The wedding suite reflected their aesthetic with the use of clean typography and elegant lettering.

Event Design: Stefanie Miles Events
Calligraphy: Julie Song Ink
Floral Design: Bows and Arrows

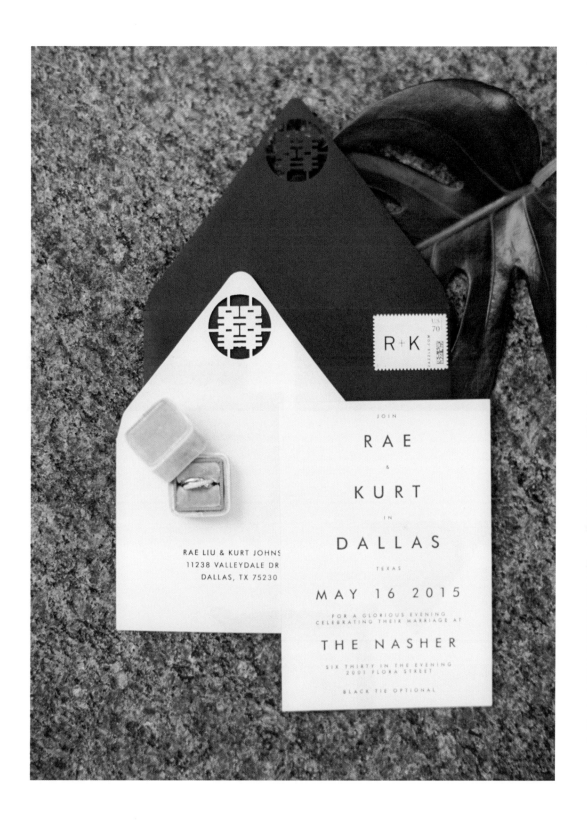

Daniela & Klaus's
Message in the Bottle

Design: Bureau Rabensteiner

Shabby chic with a squeeze of lemon – this is how the stationery design for the wedding of Daniela and Klaus was meant to feel. The ceremony and festivities took place at a beautiful location in Mallorca, Spain. Instead of just working with typography and paper, the design team put their focus very much on the still life photography. They boldly created a "message in the bottle" key visual to get people in the right mood and excited about the couple's special day weeks before the wedding.

THE SWEETEST DAY

D&K
Daniela Klaus

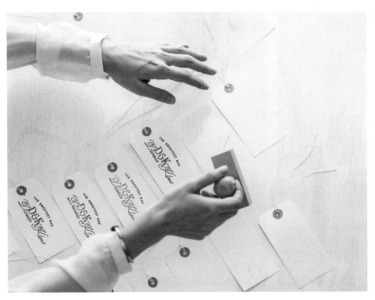

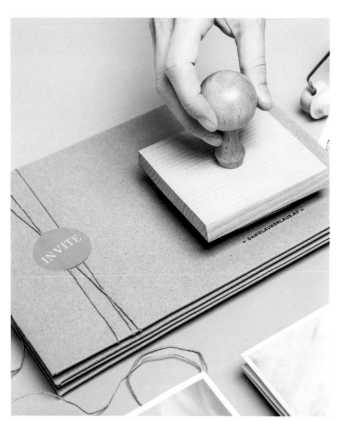

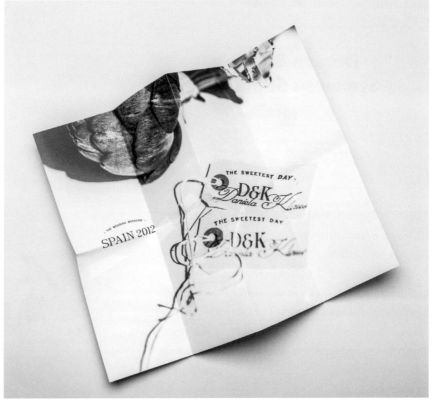

Doreen & Uwe's Symbiosis Stationery

Design: Doreen Baldauf-Uhlmann
Photography: Doreen Baldauf-Uhlmann,
Marlen Mieth

The bride, Dorreen, designed the wedding stationery for her own special day. With its combination of a clean font and hand lettering, the stationery reflected how well the couple's different characters fit together – he is very organized and she is the creative chaos. The color of the small church that was their venue was the inspiration for the coloring. To fit a modern style, each paper item only uses white lettering against a background of a single color. The layout is clean and simple, allowing the hand lettering to stand out.

. HOORAY .

DOREEN UND UWE

20. JUNI 2015

·1·
DOREEN & UWE
ELKE & UWE
ANGELIKA & JÜRGEN
NADINE
OMA INGE
RENATE & HANNO

2
KATHRIN
CAROLIN
DOREEN S.
SEBASTIAN V.
SABINE
CHRISTOPH

3
JULIA
INGO
OSKAR
ANTJE G.
GREGOR
ERWIN
JENS

4
LARS
ANTJE P.
EMMA
MARCEL
INES R.
FELICITAS

5
SILVANA
RENÉ F.
LUISE
RALF
KATRIN
ANDRÉ
JULI & TONI

6
MICHAEL
ANTJE B.
MIA
THOMAS
SANDRA
EMILIA

7
ISABELL
DANIEL
NICOLE
CHRISTIAN
ERIK
LENA
MARLEN

8
ANGELA
DIETER
CAROLA
BIRGIT
MARIO
INES S.
RENÉ S.

9
NIKLAS
ANNE
SILVIA
SEBASTIAN C.
SÖREN

**DEINEN SITZ FINDEST DU HIER
ABER DEIN PLATZ IST AUF DER TANZFLÄCHE**

.HOORAY.

DOREEN und **UWE**

feiern das Fest ihrer Liebe

am **20** sten

im

JUNI

Dieser Tag soll etwas ganz besonderes werden. »Das Versprechen füreinander« geben wir uns um 13:30 Uhr in der Kirche Limbach. Anschließend wollen wir gemeinsam lachen, feiern und unter dem Sternenhimmel tanzen. Mit euch zusammen wird es ein Fest der Liebe, Freude und Familie.

Beschreibe ein lustiges 20€ Date.

Doreen & Uwe · 20. Juni 2015

packt eure Taschen und feiert

WIR FEIEN MIT

Konfetti

SPASS UND

VERRÜCKTEN

Tanzmoves

D

M

.MARLÉN.

Schön, dass du mit uns feierst.

Eure Liebe bringt Licht in unser Leben

Hand in Hand ein Leben lang

menu

7

unsere Lieben

NIKLAS und ANNE

kommt und feiert mit uns.

Niklas & Anne Schneider

.HOORAY.

DOREEN und **UWE**

feiern das Fest ihrer Liebe

unsere Lieben

NIKLAS und ANNE

kommt und feiert mit uns.

Dieser Tag soll etwas ganz besonderes werden. »Das Versprechen füreinander« geben wir uns um 13:30 Uhr in der Kirche Limbach. Anschließend wollen wir gemeinsam lachen, feiern und unter dem Sternenhimmel tanzen. Mit euch zusammen wird es ein Fest der Liebe, Freude und Familie.

Carley & Brandon's
Winter Wonderland Suite

Design: Coral Pheasant Stationery
Photography: Carla Ten Eyck

The styled shoot taken in Vermont encompassed all of the best parts of winter – cozy fabrics, interesting textures, fluffy white snow, comforting treats and warm snuggles. It was all about snow, sparkle, and sweet sentiments. For the paper story, texture was translated through mixed typefaces, varied borders, and a herringbone patterned envelope liner. The quirky serif font paired with a more traditional serif typeface created an endearing contrast. A laser cut snowflake belly band added dimension and further emphasized the winter theme.

YOU ARE

cordially invited

TO CELEBRATE THE WEDDING OF

CARLEY LEIGH WATKINS

&

BRANDON MILES CAESER

SATURDAY AFTERNOON JANUARY SIXTH

two thousand fourteen

AT FOUR O'CLOCK

THE CHESSER HOMESTEAD

weston, vermont

Billingsworth – Ikat Pattern Suite

Design: MaeMae & Co.

Billingsworth is one of MaeMae's wedding collection characters. These suites were created to give clients fun, fashion-forward, and totally ready-to-order options when choosing their wedding stationery. All of the MaeMae wedding characters have a mix and match quality with lots of texture through the patterns, illustrations, and type treatment. Billingsworth is a mix of flat printed and letterpress printed pieces with a modern ikat pattern.

CFR

39048
BLANCA BLVD
SONOMA
CALIFORNIA
95476

CFR

CATHERINE
AND
REMINGTON
OCTOBER 10, 2015

❖

FIRST COURSE
SMOKED CHESTNUT BISQUE SOUP
micro intensity

SECOND COURSE
PUMPKIN AGNOLOTTI.
BUERRE FONDUE

DESSERT
BUTTERSCOTCH PUDDING
THYME PANNA COTTA.
SWEET POTATO BRITTLE.

KINDLY RESPOND BY
THE TWELFTH OF SEPTEMBER

M_____

___ ACCEPTS ___ REGRETS

Céline & Emmanuel's
Suite with Pins

Design: Chloé Noret
Photography: Pedro Loustau

The team created all of the decorations for this wedding with only lace and satin ribbon, clear glass yoghurt pots, creative paper choices, candles, a few crafty skills, and a bit of time. A candy bar with beautiful jars was designed to please children and grown-ups alike. Save-the-dates were printed locally on a beautiful soft paper. Pins were used to indicate whether guests were the bride's or the groom's family or friends. Each color stood for each "group": bride's family (pink), groom's family (blue), bride and groom's friends (green), friends of the families (grey).

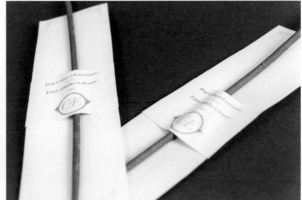

Camélia

Lauren & Ben's NYC Wedding Suite

Design: And Here We Are
Photography: And Here We Are, Amber Gress

For this modern black, white, and gold NYC wedding invitation, the design team combined letterpress printing with gold foil stamping onto double-thick cotton paper. The RSVP became a true postcard, digitally printed onto glossy stock to stand apart from the letterpress pieces. The team had a little fun with the map card, including tiny illustrations of the weekend's events. To give the package a sleek and modern feel, the team created a patterned wrap enclosed in a translucent envelope in lieu of a simple envelope with liner. The wrap folded diagonally around the cards and was sealed with a custom gold wax seal. The team later created menus, die cut escort cards, custom placemats, and used the couple's "logo" on things like tote bags and matchbooks.

OUR WEDDING WEEKEND

SATURDAY, SEPTEMBER 5TH
WELCOME PARTY – DINNER & DRINKS
6PM / 54 WEST 40TH STREET, NEW YORK, NY

SUNDAY, SEPTEMBER 6TH
WEDDING CEREMONY & RECEPTION
5:30PM / THE FOUNDRY
42-38 9TH STREET, LONG ISLAND CITY, NY

MONDAY, SEPTEMBER 7TH
FAREWELL BURGERS & SHAKES
11AM–1PM / SHAKE SHACK
MADISON SQUARE PARK, NEW YORK, NY

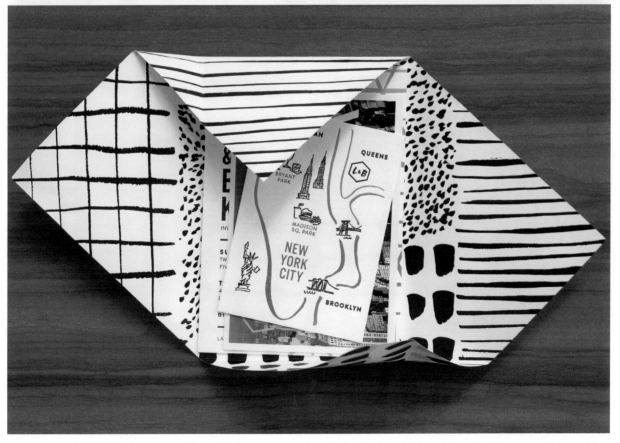

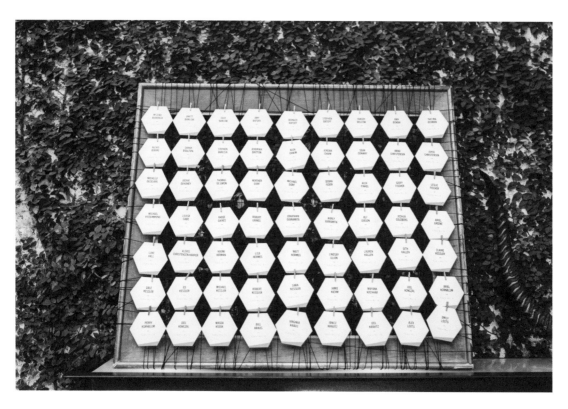

Mark & Charlotte's
Spice Suite

Design: Charlotte Fosdike

Charlotte designed this clean and elegant wedding suite for her own wedding. The suite gave their guests a small taste of them as a couple and shared with them the treasures of new and exciting flavors. It delivered beyond visual representation by including interactive packaging to appeal to touch and a mixed array of spices in the packets to delight through scent and taste. Charlotte and Mark assembled the suite themselves by handcrafting small brown boxes, in which they placed seven individually-designed and crafted packets of spices as well as invitations with wedding details and further information.

WELCOME TO THE WEDDING
of

...

MARK
and
CHARLOTTE

...

Saturday 18th of February 2012
Circle of Oaks, Corner of John Fisher
Avenue and Victoria Street,
Gumeracha at 2pm.

WE'RE NOT ON FACEBOOK.
so please sign our guest book.

dried chillies

SWEET
PAPRIKA

DEAR STEPHEN AND REBEKAH JONES

Here is a gift of spices that will give you a taste of who we are.
We've chosen seven of our favourite flavours - those with which
that we've enjoyed whiffing and those that remind us of times we
As you probably know, we're rather adventurous people; we love to
and meet new people.

WHEN WE'RE TOGETHER, WE'LL SOMETIMES COMPARE EACH OTHER TO
MARK SAYS HOT AND DELIGHTFUL, CHARLOTTE SAYS FULL OF FLAVOU
AND AMAZING ADVENTURES.

We both love that exoticness that the first taste delivers, as well as the mysteri
ride that the spice takes us on as it matures in our palette - be it a slow sweetenin
a stimulating burn or a surprising softening of tang which eases the bitterness of the
We think that it can represent our journey together, past to r   nt to future, satura
our lives in colour, variety and adventure. With this little   can have a taste of
our perspective. Go on, we dare you to give some of t'   are pretty tasty,
especially with food.

So, to help celebrate our passion for eac'
Annie Heidenreich, together with P   ife, Boyd and
to our wedding.   nvite you

MARK
and
CHARLOTTE

PLEASE
RSVP

                                                         MONY
                                                           m
INSTRUCTIONS   cle
Ok so, all you need to do is tick the   er
boxes, write out your info and send   et
it back. Pretty simple really.

If you are a bit low on cash and don't
have the spare sixty cents we totally
understand. Just text Annie or email
her with your attendance and dietary
requirements.

DETAILS
Email: annie@inandoutliving.com.au
Mobile: 0419 831 041

ADDRESS
Post Office Box 808 Mt Barker
South Australia 5251

SZUCHUAN
PEPPER

GROUND
GINGER

MOROCCAN
SUMAC

SWEET
PAPRIKA

CRUSHED
CHILLI

CURRY
LEAVES

CINNAMON
QUILLS

Mayra & Jorge's
2-typefaces Invitation

Design: Mayra Monobe

The designer used two different typefaces – a serif and a sans-serif – to communicate the different personalities of the couple. Besides the invitation with all relevant info, a booklet with two covers to explain the couple's lives, gift cards with photos of the honeymoon destination, and thank you notes were also created.

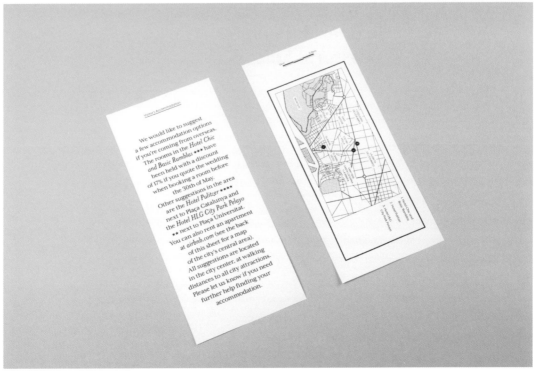

Heather & Taylor's
Pastoral Suite

Design: Caitlin Workman

Caitlin collaborated directly with the couple to help distill their inspiration into a modern, sophisticated design, developing their ideas into an alluring and distinctive wedding suite. The goal was to create a consistent design that would express ornate elegance while being mindful of a strict timeline and budget. With this in mind a single gold metallic ink was used across the suite, including in the self-mailing RSVP cards, which eliminated the

need for additional materials and allowed for a cost-effective, one-color print production. The intricate design reflects whimsy, timelessness, and pastoral elements inspired by the overall thematic direction. Decorative elements were inspired by art deco line work and carefully designed to look like lace. Other special touches included letterpress printing and gold foil.

Jennifer & Joshua's Star Wars Suite

Stationery Design: MaeMae & Co.
Photography: MaeMae & Co.,
Cacá Santoro Photography

A custom made suite for the reception of a downtown Los Angeles wedding. The bride and groom incorporated their love for Star Wars through their wedding. The result included Stormtrooper escorts, Death Star coasters, and hints of Star Wars in the music, programs, table names, and signage.

Thank You
FOR YOUR GENEROSITY!
PLEASE PLACE GIFTS HERE
AND CARDS INSIDE THE
DEATH STAR

signature
COCKTAILS
GINGER MOJITO
RUM, FRESH LIME JUICE, GINGER & MINT SIMPLE SYRUP,
AND TOPPED WITH A SPLASH OF GINGER ALE

SPICY RED CHILE-GUAVA
MARGARITA
RED CHILE-INFUSED TEQUILA, GUAVA NECTAR,
TRIPLE SEC, AND FRESH LIME JUICE

BEER
LAGER
IPA

WINE
ROSÉ
CHARDONNAY
PINOT NOIR
CABERNET SAUVIGNON

J + J

PLEASE
PICK A PAGE AND
LEAVE YOUR M
ON THIS NEW CHAPTER
OUR EPIC JOURNEY

9.20.14

TA

MANDA

TABLE

JEDI KNIGHT

dinner
MENU

JENNIFER + JOSHUA

LOS ELEVEN PENTHOUSE · LOS ANGELES · 6.28.2014

SALAD
Baby Arugula, Creamy Burrata,
Roasted Grapes · Brown Butter Balsamic

ENTREE
Grilled Sea Bass with Crushed
Almonds · Chili Lemon Dressing
or
Montreal Crusted Filet of Beef
with a Bordelaise Jus

Roasted Asparagus Spears with
Sea Salt · Yukon Gold Potato Puree

WEDDING CAKE
FROM THE BUTTER END CAKERY

Blueberry Walnut Cake
with Sweet Lemon Buttercream

Chocolate Almond Cherry Cake
with Cherry Cream Cheese Buttercream

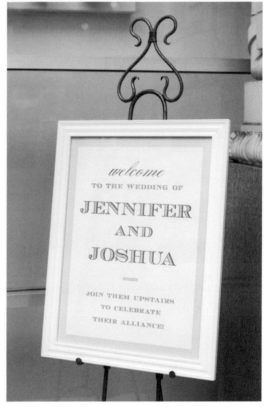

welcome

TO THE WEDDING OF

JENNIFER

AND

JOSHUA

JOIN THEM UPSTAIRS

TO CELEBRATE

THEIR ALLIANCE!

Nádia & Pedro's Mint Green Suite

Design: Constança Soromenho

Nádia and Pedro's big day was fun and creative, and the wedding suite matched the ceremony's tone. Alongside the invitation, the team designed an RSVP card where guests could fill in their own song suggestion. Pins were created for the best men and bridesmaids, while disposable cameras on every table encouraged guests to capture unforgettable moments.

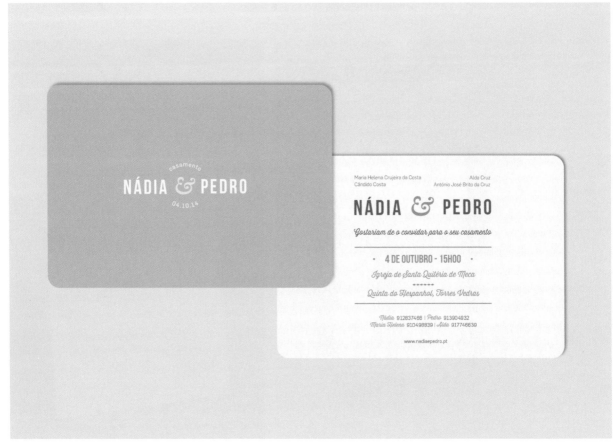

Anisa & Michele's Musical Note Suite

Design: Giorgia Smiraglia

Inspired by the countryside environment, this suite set the perfect tone for Anisa and Michele's wedding. The young couple wanted a rustic yet elegant wedding atmosphere that represented their personalities and their passion for music. For this reason, the logo borrows aesthetics from the design of musical notes; even the decorative elements were designed to recall a staff. This informed the rest of the design including invitations, table cards, menus, the wedding table plan, and the party favor parchments. The color palette was inspired by the location, a grassy garden full of daisies. All of the materials were printed on a recycled uncoated paper.

Madeline & Marshall's Oversized Invitation

Design: MaeMae & Co.

The wedding featured a fun oversized invitation and modern mix and match fonts. Die cut menus and programs added variety to the shape of the paper goods.

CEREMONY
KISSING
MISTER&MISSUS
COCKTAILS AND APPETIZERS
YUM DINNER YUM
CHAMPAGNE TOASTS
TUNES
DANCING... MORE CHAMPAGNE
CAKE CUTTING
LOVE
SWEET LOVE

14

FIELD SALAD
FREE RANGE
CHICKEN
WITH VIDALIA ONION RELISH
SALSA AND TEMPURA
CAKE SWEET CAKE

FIELD SALAD
FREE RANGE
CHICKEN
WITH VIDALIA ONION RELISH
SALSA AND TEMPURA
CAKE SWEET CAKE

M IS FOR MACAROON
M IS FOR MACAROON
M IS FOR MACAROON
M IS FOR MACAROON

MADDEN

FIELD SALAD
FREE RANGE
CHICKEN
WITH VIDALIA ONION RELISH
SALSA AND TEMPURA
CAKE SWEET CAKE

Winston – Coral Suite

Design: MaeMae & Co.

Winston is MaeMae & Co.'s punchy interpretation of
a seaside wedding. Coral-shaped graphics are made
decidedly modern through the use of a red and purple
color scheme.

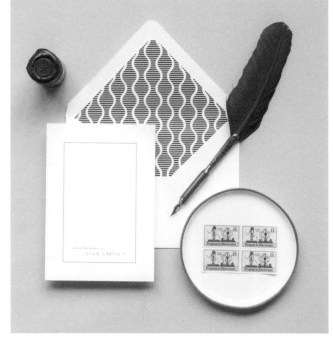

WELCOME *to the*

GRAND
CANYON
STATE

it's time to party!

Together
with their families

ASTRID NELSON
and WINSTON MARKS

invite you to celebrate with them as they are married

SATURDAY, APRIL TWENTY-EIGHTH

Two thousand twelve at Five in the evening

The Bosque Tree / 10226 E. 56Th Street

Phoenix, Arizona Dinner party following at the Olde Pink House

2

WEEKEND
FESTIVITIES

Welcome Fiesta
Saturday, February 16, 2013
at 7 pm
Fire Pit Lawn

Farewell Brunch
Monday February 18, 2013
at 11 AM
Norma's

The wedding and all
weekend events will take place at
THE PARKER | PALM SPRINGS
4200 E. Palm Canyon Drive, Palm Springs, CA

PLEASE
REPLY BY

April Seventh, 2012

_____

_____

○ happily accepts
○ regretfully declines

ASTRID & WINSTON
APRIL 28, 2012 *Phoenix, Arizona*

BRIDAL PARTY

Parents of the Bride
MR. & MRS. GREG NELSON

Parents of the Groom
MR. & MRS. BRANDON
MARKS

Grandparents of the Groom
WALTER & FLO MARKS

Bridesmaids
SAM NELSON
TRACY HUDSON
KATE LEE
TATE MARKS

Groomsmen
BRAD WILSON
ROB MARTINEZ
TIM NELSON
PHIL MARKS

Flower Girls
BAILEY MARKS
MARY MARKS

Officiant
REV. BLAKE KENLEY

CEREMONY

Bridal Procession
WEDDING MARCH

Opening Prayer
MR. BRANDON MARKS
FATHER OF THE GROOM

Exchange Of Vows

Exchange Of Rings

Special Music
GIVE BLESSINGS TO THIS DAY
SUNG BY JULIE-ANNE SMITH

AT LAST
SUNG BY TATE MARKS

Blessing
GREG NELSON
FATHER OF THE BRIDE

Pronouncement

Recessional
TRUMPET VOLUNTARY

We want to thank all of you for being here today. It means so much that
you're able to be a part of our special day. Each one of you has played a
significant part in our lives and we are so grateful. Thank you!!

Kelsy & Kevin's
Vintage Suite

Design: Kelsy Stromski (Refinery 43)
Photography: Cindy Giovagnoli

The designer created a suite of stationery for her own wedding held at the botanical gardens on the coast of Maine. The natural beauty of the gardens, a touch of vintage elegance, nautical and navy themes, and romance became her inspiration. From custom wood stamps and wax seals to cotton stationery, she used a variety of techniques within a realistic budget. The design turned out setting just the right tone for the day and creating the special touches she wanted for her guests. The stationery and wedding day were featured in the Real Maine Weddings' January 2014 issue and WellWed Magazine Blog.

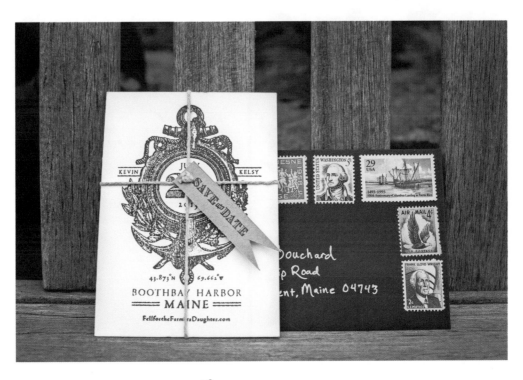

Ashley & Edwin's Bushveld-inspired Stationery

Design: Lize-Marie Dreyer
(Aurora Creative Studio)

A South African Bushveld inspired wedding stationery featuring South African kingfisher birds as well as indigenous plants.

Kat & Tom's Stationery with a Map

Design: Tom Pitts
Photography: James Donnelly, Duke Studios

Tom designed the wedding stationery for his own wedding with five different paper stocks, four print techniques, three sections, and two folding methods. The main invite was printed on stained laserply and screen printed in white. The milkman's wallet is GF Smith duplex and was custom folded by Kat. The map was litho printed and used a simple origami technique. All were sealed in a lovely hand-stamped envelope with a string and button closure.

Kim & Will's
All-caps Invitation

Design: Sylvain Toulouse

Kim and Will were married in a beautiful old church in Maidenhead, England in 2013. For the special occasion, they wanted a custom invitation to send to their relatives and close friends that would represent them in a soft, contemporary, and fashionable way. The designer used a tinted semi-transparent vellum envelope to hold the distinct RSVP cards, which were designed with a mix of modern all-caps and classic typefaces.

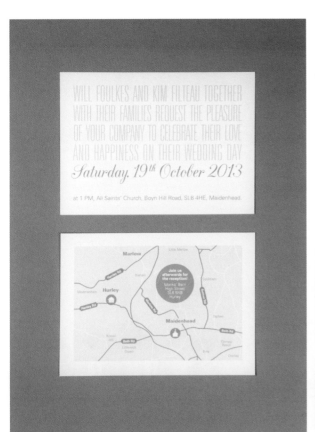

WILL FOULKES AND KIM FILTEAU TOGETHER
WITH THEIR FAMILIES REQUEST THE PLEASURE
OF YOUR COMPANY TO CELEBRATE THEIR LOVE
AND HAPPINESS ON THEIR WEDDING DAY
Saturday, 19th October 2013

at 1 PM, All Saints' Church, Boyn Hill Road, SL6 4HE, Maidenhead.

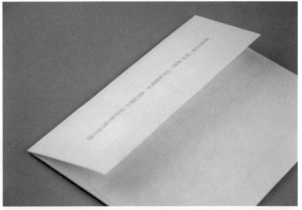

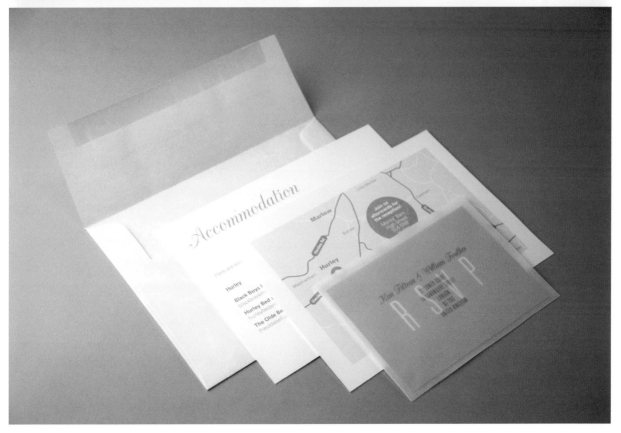

Jon & Nicole's "Hooray" Suite

Design: Jon Jackson

The couple designed the wedding materials for their own wedding. They started with the save-the-date coasters. Each guest got an enthusiastic phrase (like "Hooray!" and "Fuck Yeah!") with wedding date and location details. For the invitation, Jon made an 18×24 inch silk screen poster invitation showing the places he and Nicole had traveled and things they had done together in three colors (blue, red, and gold). Each poster was rolled up and mailed in a triangular tube, with a different custom greeting stamped on the outside. All of these variations gave each guest a unique invitation set. At the wedding, guests found their seats through colored buttons created with key visuals from the poster. At their seats, guests were greeted with custom tote bags, again printed in one of the three colors. In the end, 3 different thank you cards were created to close out their wedding.

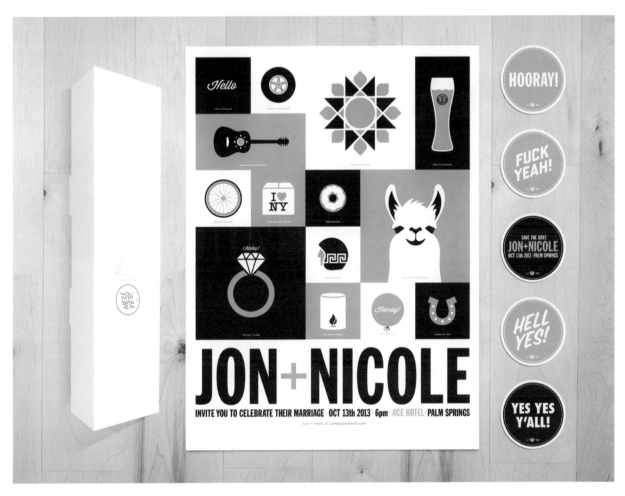

Hermie – Swedish Pattern Suite

Design: MaeMae & Co.

Hermie is one of MaeMae's wedding collection characters, inspired by Swedish patterns and iconography with a fresh pink and grey palette.

TOGETHER WITH THEIR FAMILIES

CAROLYN PARK

AND

AARON GILLESPIE

INVITE YOU TO CELEBRATE THEIR WEDDING ON

09.27.14

AT FIVE IN THE EVENING AT THE LANGHAM HOTEL

PASADENA, A

HEMINGWAYS

PLEASE SAY YES

BEFORE AUGUST FIRST

M _____

yes!   sorry

Maja & Nathan's Monogram Suite

Design: Nathan Parker

Nathan created the wedding suite and identity for his own wedding to Maja, and set the entire basis and theme for the special day. The identity featured a subtle logo using the first letters of their names. It was strong, vibrant, and very personal for Nathan, and they were both very proud and pleased with its impact and results.

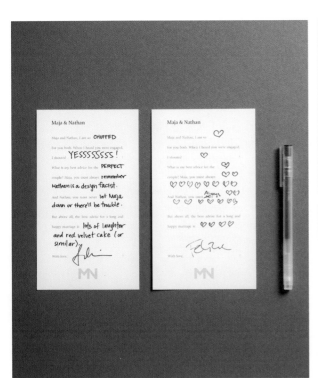

Anna & Kyle's Gallery Show

Design: Anna O'Connell

Anna and Kyle were married in a private ceremony, followed by a gallery show of art objects they had made for each other over the course of their relationship. Their stationery suite for this celebration consists of a zine, which served as a guide to the event, as well as a save-the-date, invitation, RSVP card, thank you note, and takeaway gift set of four prints. Additionally, an enlarged,

colorized version of the invitation was displayed as part of their exhibition. The takeaway and the colorized invitation were digitally printed, and the remaining components of the suite were made with a Risograph machine. The patterns referenced among the suite are composed of objects that represented the event and their relationship: music, food, and their many plants.

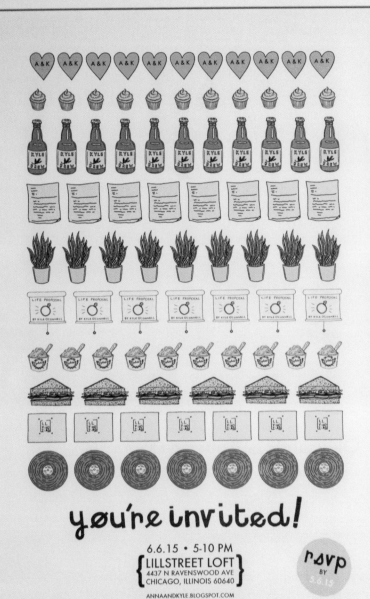

Oleksandr & Andriana's
Pinecone Invitation

Design: Andriana Chunis

The designer created this work for her own forest-themed wedding. She used a pinecone as the main visual element and created a linocut effect to reflect the theme. As making stamps is laborious, she imitated the imprints by using Photoshop. She used different line thicknesses to give the illustrations an intentional shabby feel that looked like real stamps. Information including date, place, and time was enlarged and emphasized, while illustrations were used to divide the invitation into separate blocks. She used decorative string to tie the invitation closed as the finishing touch.

13:30 вінчання у храмі Ольги та Єлизавети

16:00 святкування у ресторані "Вілла Австрія"

Kirstin & Pablo's Invitation with Beach Icons

Design: The Pick of the Crab

An invitation designed for a wedding held in Punta de Lobos (Wolves Point), Chile with illustrations resembling beach items.

Kirsten & Bobo ❤ 8/3/2014 ❤ Punta de Lobos

YUMMY

APPETIZERS

* AHI TUNA POKE SERVED OVER BOK CHOY LEAVES
* HAI CRAB CAKE
* BRUSCHETTAS OF OLIVE CAVIAR TOPPED WITH GOAT CHEESE

MAIN COURSE

* RED WINE PARRILLADA WITH RYE CABERNET SAUVIGNON WINE
* SELECTION OF CAPRA WINE WITH CABERNET SAUVIGNON WINE
* FRUIT JUICES & WATER
* ORGANIC GREEN SALAD WITH HOUSE DRESSING
* LOCAL KELP SALAD WITH LEMON VINAIGRETTE
* HUMMUS WR LOBA GRANO
* BREAD WR

OR {
* SEAM FL STUFFED WITH CREAM CHEESE, RUCOLA, AND PARMA HAM.
* SEARED FL BAKED WITH CHORIZO, SERVED WITH BREAD BEAN PURÉE.
* SOUTHERN LIME ICOD GRILLED IN PISTACHIO CRUST, SERVED WITH
* BASMATI RICE PERFUMED WITH KAFFIR LIME LEAVES, LEMON ZEST AND
* FRESH GINGER.

DESSERT

* CREME BRULEE
* CHOCOLATE & RASPBERRY SABLE DOUGH CAKE
* BAKED COCONUT MILK WITH CARAMEL AND CARDAMOM
* MERINGUE PASTRY WITH ALMONDS & PASSION FRUIT MOUSSE OVER WHITE CHOCOLATE

DIGESTIF

MINT ✳ AMARETTO ✳ COFFEE LIQUOR ✳ FERNET BRANCA ✳ MIXED DRINKS

LATE NIGHTER

* PORK SANDWICHES WITH MERLOT ONIONS AND HOLLANDAISE SAUCE
* SQUASH WITH JEREZ-WINE SHOTS

Bridget & Preston's
Laser Cut Invitation

Design: Sofia Invitations and Prints
Photography: Mel Nocks Photography

The designer was invited to participate in this style shoot with Wedding 101 in Greenville, South Carolina. The theme was modern with pops of bright colors in fuchsia and gold. Laser cut wedding invitations, signage, gold escort names, and a cameo silhouette were created.

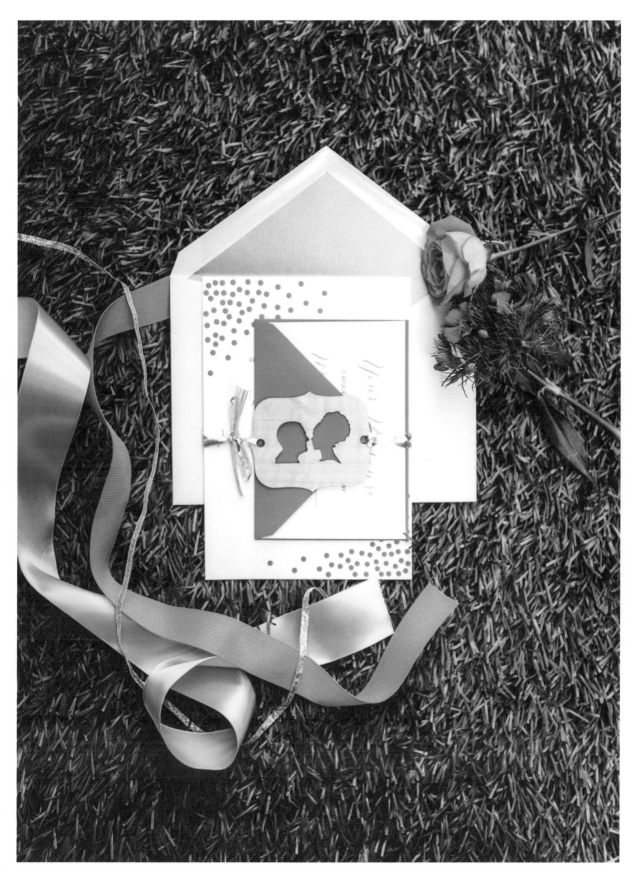

Maeve & Graham's
Farmland Suite

Design: Coral Pheasant Stationery
Photography: Nancy Ray Photography

The couple married on a plot of farmland where they would
build their forever home. The stationery suite features a
wash of pastel colors and cheerful typography on diamond
shaped cards. True to form, the designer incorporated
vintage stamps in nontraditional ways. There was also a
map of the couple's farmland, pointing out key wedding
day locations as well as the site of their future home.

Map Illustration: Social Alchemy

MR. AND MRS. THOMAS RAMSEY
*invite you to share in the joy of the marriage
uniting their daughter*

*Maeve Graham
Aubrey to Orville
Ramsey Sanfield*

SATURDAY, JUNE SEVENTEENTH, TWO THOUSAND SEVENTEEN
three in the afternoon at the future Sanfield homestead
4125 Dogwood Hill
Clinton, North Carolina
DINNER ON THE FARM TO FOLLOW

WATERMELON

FOR MORE INFORMATION
about our special day please visit
www | *Maeve and Graham* | com

MR. AND MRS. THOMAS RAMSEY
Beamon Woods Road
Clinton, North Carolina
28328

*Mr. and Mrs. Brian Donahue
804 Old Tucker Road
Stone Mountain, Georgia
30121*

RED ONION &
BLUEBERRIES

PLEASE SAY
yes

tickled pink ○ | ○ *aw schucks*

REPLY BY MAY
fifteenth

Wedding:
28 NOV

Party:
5 DEC

ANNA & ALEXEY

2015

Anna & Alexey's
Late Autumn
Wedding Invitation

Design: Anna Shuvalova

The invitation and the guest book were created for the wedding held in the late autumn in St. Petersburg, Russia. Gridelin, brown, and snow-blue colors made one feel the spirit and the mood of this time of the year with poetically dismal weather, dull skies, and naked trees all around. Pencil-drawn illustrations were created especially for the project. Combined with the letter A (the first letters of the couple's names), they became the key pillars of the event's identity.

Paula & Bryan's Vineyard-inspired Stationery

Design: Belinda Love Lee

The wedding invites were inspired by the location – the couple were married on a vineyard. The designer hand-illustrated the vines and flowers in watercolor and paired them alongside fancy hand lettering. The envelopes were penned by the bride to give a personal touch for each guest. The programs designed for the day were not only pretty but very functional, as the designer added handles to make them into fans for the hot day's occasion.

Helena & Jan's Provence-styled Suite

Design: Tessa Persoons
Photography: Yann Deschepper

Tessa designed a whole set of wedding stationery including invitations, save-the-dates, menu cards, and signs for Jan and Helena's romantic wedding held in the south of France. She went for a Provence style with naive hand-drawn illustrations and toned down colors to reflect both the beautiful natural surroundings and charming atmosphere created by the setting.

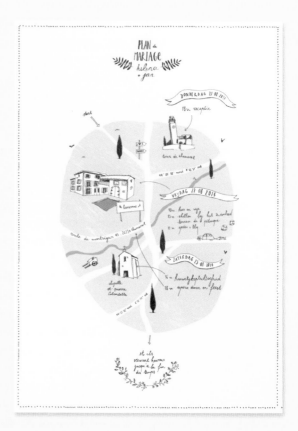

Geoffrey & Jaimie's
Fish Hook Invitation

Design: Kathy Ager

The ceremony was held in Sointula, an isolated village on Malcolm Island in British Columbia, Canada. The designer created custom illustrations with silver foil details and a fish hook monogram to reflect the location. Finally, the invites were tied together and presented like a bundle of treasures pulled from the sea.

Fly Fishing Invitation

Design: Cast Calligraphy

The Fly Fishing invitation is one of the suites from Cast Calligraphy which was created for outdoor enthusiast couples. Bozeman is a recreational haven for many people and fly fishing there is a world-class experience. It's also a destination town for many and an ideal setting for a wedding. This design is classic and simple with a touch of modern elements and whimsical calligraphy.

Cleo & Dan's
Italy Meets New York Suite

Design: And Here We Are
Photography: And Here We Are, Jessica Schmitt

Inspired by wedding theme "Italy meets New York," this suite was a meld of Italian and classic New York aesthetics. For the paper goods, the team created a twist on traditional calligraphic script combined with Bodoni type, digitally printed on lush cotton paper. To contrast the classic and clean look of the invitations, they paired them with a bright yellow envelope lined with a cute rosemary pattern.

Sarah & David's Invitation with Spray Technics

Design: FØLSOM Studio

Based in Paris, Imprimerie du Marais is well known for its high quality and refined printing services. In 2015, the company created La Belle Histoire, an e-shop selling sets of wedding invitations. The brand expresses the team's artistic direction, while the graphic design of these pieces are inspired by the world of fashion and luxury. Thus the team experimented with the expression of gesture in an artistic way, using spray techniques on paper that they reworked and digitized. Moreover, they designed a unique ampersand in order to express the beauty of the union of two lovers, drawing smooth curves and strokes evoking haute-couture creations. The set is printed with pink-gold foil on a night blue paper and a pink iridescent paper to create a strong contrast and highlight the shining flakes.

FRANÇOIS

&

KEL

SERAIENT HEUREUX DE VOUS
AVOIR À LEURS CÔTÉS
À L'OCCASION DE LEUR MARIAGE
LE 29 AOÛT 2015

REQUEST THE HONOR
OF YOUR PRESENCE
AT THEIR WEDDING
ON AUGUST 29TH 2015

☐ SUPRÊME DE POULET ASIATIQUE
ASIAN INSPIRED CHICKEN SUPRÊME

☐ FILET DE PORC LAQUÉ À L'ÉRABLE
MAPLE GLAZED PORK MEDALLIONS

MERCI DE RÉPONDRE AVANT LE 30 JUIN
KINDLY RESPOND BY JUNE 30TH

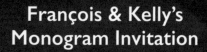

François & Kelly's
Monogram Invitation

Design: Studio Caserne, Atelier BangBang

François and Kelly are very good friends of the designer. For their wedding gift, the team gave them a formal interpretation of their initials. It was screen printed 200 times to invite their friends and relatives.

Jason & Yvette's Invitation with a Booklet

Design: The Hungry Workshop
Photography: Nikole Ramsay

The couple was engaged and married in a well-loved surf shack in Separation Creek. Their invitation is a collection of stocks, finishes, and techniques. The envelope appears small, but is actually an A3 sheet of newsprint, letterpress printed by hand in a soft blue ink on the team's Asbern Proof Press. Inside is a small booklet, with several sheet sizes thread-stitched along spine with a mixture of printing techniques. The booklet tells the couple's story and is peppered with facts about the pair. The invitation is informative, direct, honest, and personal, just like the couple themselves.

Jason

& Yvette

met during French class,
in the 7th grade.

Jason

asked Yvette to marry him on
the beach, just before low tide,
at Separation Creek on Saturday,
10 March 2012.

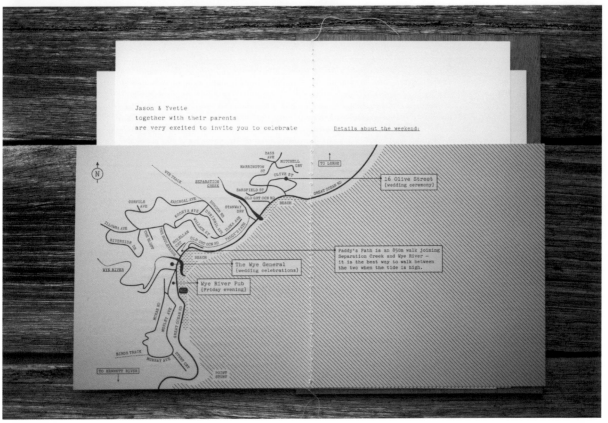

Jason & Yvette
together with their parents
are very excited to invite you to celebrate   Details about the weekend:

16 Olive Street
[wedding ceremony]

The Wye General
[wedding celebrations]

Wye River Pub
[Friday evening]

Paddy's Path is an 850m walk joining
Separation Creek and Wye River —
it is the best way to walk between
the two when the tide is high.

Stephanie and Dustin's
Baja California Suite

Design: Yonder Design
Photography: Josh Gruetzmacher

Created for a beach wedding in Cabo San Lucas, Mexico, this invitation suite embodied the casual refinement of Baja California. The save-the-date was letterpress printed in three colors and sewn together with a tri-folded backing and screen-printed linen cover. The piece was held together with a silk ribbon and mailed within a cotton envelope sealed with the couple's monogram. The invitation carried a similar color palette, but used a white-washed piece of wood as the backing for the main invitation. Turquoise dyed deerskin lacing was wrapped around the wood as an accent and helped to keep the reply envelopes and additional cards on the backside in place. The couple's monogram was laser engraved into the wood on the reverse, and all of the elements were wrapped in a linen sleeve with a wax seal as a closure.

STEPHANIE & DUSTIN

220 NICE LANE · APT 116

NEWPORT BEACH · CALIFORNIA 92663

Mitchell and Kyle's
Masculine Suite

Design: Yonder Design
Photography: Jesse Leake

This masculine suite was highlighted by the laser engraved slate tiles that served as the main invitation. Slate is quite soft and takes very well to laser engraving. To protect the tiles, a custom leather wrap was created, which also held the additional pieces together. The other cards were kept clean and simple with a modern geometric pattern and a mixture of script and serif fonts. Each guest at the event had their own tags engraved for keepsakes when they left.

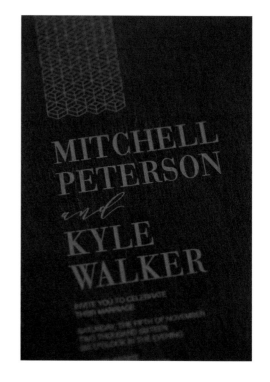

Merielle and Bob's Floral Save-the-Date

Design: Yonder Design
Photography: Jesse Leake

This floral save-the-date is based around the beautiful still life photograph in the liner from Addie Juell. The main text is letterpress printed on double thick cotton stock, and mounted to a 4-ply museum board used for fine art framing. The back side of the black board includes a blind deboss of a floral pattern, bleeding off the edge. The piece is finished with burgundy silk ribbon and a wax seal incorporating the couple's monogram. Each piece was mailed in a black envelope with calligraphy for the addressing.

Emily & David's Gem Suite

Design: And Here We Are
Photography: Katie Osgood

The designer was especially inspired by bright, rich jewel tones and shapes for this wedding. She used a big brush pen loaded with ink to create bold, modern script lettering and patterns, then digitized them to combine them with custom watercolor-filled gem artwork and clean typography. Each piece was digitally printed and then cut down into gem shapes. Pairing these pieces with an assortment of gem toned envelopes lined with an inky brush pattern gave it one more burst of color. The team extended these visuals to create vertical gem-shaped menus, square favor tags, and round coasters for the event.

Charmaine & Patrick's Mini Guide

Design: Charmaine Choi
Cover Flower Illustration: Annie Lim

Charmaine wanted to create a keepsake for their guests coming to their wedding in New York. As most of the guests were from out of town, the couple created a mini guide to New York through their eyes. This doubled as the invite, which worked out perfectly for its collaboration with Scout Books and Raaka Chocolates.

Family Style Menu

APPETIZER
Burrata speck, arugula, crisps

ENTRÉES
Roasted Chicken *Smoked pancetta, spinach, celery root, leeks*
Shoulder *Beer-braised red onions*

SIDES
Roasted Pumpkin *Olive oil, sea salt, herbs*
Roasted Potatoes *Aleppo, olive oil, sea salt, herbs*
Roasted Baby Carrots* *Shaved beets, toasted walnuts, raisin vinaigrette*
Baked Cauliflower *Garlic cream sauce, rosemary breadcrumbs, Parmigiano*

DESSERTS
Chocolate Pudding *Whipped cream, olive oil, sea salt*
Buttermilk Panna Cotta* *Pear compote, toasted pistachios*

Purslane

Chef Arden Lewis

*contains nuts

Mike Phillips

Raaka
virgin chocolate

VANILLA
ROOIBOS
(67% cacao)

TOGETHER WITH THEIR FAMILIES
CHARMAINE & PATRICK
JOYFULLY INVITE YOU TO THEIR WEDDING,
SATURDAY, NOVEMBER 14, 2015
at **4:00**pm in the **AFTERNOON**

THE FOUNDRY
42-58 Ninth Street
Long Island City,
New York

RECEPTION
TO FOLLOW

www.CharmaineandPatrick.com

RECOVERY BRUNCH
SUNDAY, NOVEMBER 15

1PM

BUILDING ON BOND
112 Bond Street
Brooklyn, NY
11217

This is a separate invitation from the wedding.
Please RSVP to charmainechoi@gmail.com
by September 30, 2015.

REHEARSAL DINNER
FRIDAY, NOVEMBER 13

7PM

FRANKIES 457
457 Court Street
Brooklyn, NY
11231

RSVP
Please respond by September 30, 2015
You may also respond on
www.CharmaineandPatrick.com
password: elvisbk

We have reserved **2** seats for you.

○ ACCEPT WITH PLEASURE
○ DECLINE WITH REGRET

Attendee Name(s):

_____

_____

SONG REQUEST:

Artist: _____

Title: _____

Adrian & Alexandra's Peony Stationery

Design: GRAPHO_MAT
Photography: Adrian Mihaiu

Adrian and Alexandra made this invitation for their own wedding. She is slim and cute; he is chubby and cute. She likes all things flowery and colorful; he is more of a two-tone guy. Therefore they made a hand drawn illustration of a colorful peony, but in black and white. Their names made a wonderful letterplay with the initials A and A – his A is extra bold, her A is light, and together they complete each other.

Anastasia & Evgeny's
Summer Wedding Suite

Design: Anastasia Kolesnikova
Photography: Violetta Kuzmenko

This light and soft project was created for a nice summer wedding in bright, feminine colors. The rose patterns inside the envelope were made by watercolor. Hand drawn calligraphy lettering was applied to the couple's names on the invitation cover.

Anastasia & Evgeny's Winter Wedding Suite

Design: Anastasia Kolesnikova
Photography: Olga Platonova

A project for a stylish winter wedding, executed with a watercolor style. Soft and almost transparent flowers inside the envelope worked perfectly with the blue watercolor background in the invitation.

Dress-Code

for Her
a long dress in pastel colors

for Him
a dark suit with a bow tie

On the day
when "Yes"
means "Forever"

Drake – 20s-styled Suite

Design: MaeMae & Co.

Drake is one of MaeMae's wedding collection characters. It is set in the 1920s with art deco frames, patterns, and fun illustrations of party goers.

Molly & Robert's Bohemian Wedding Suite

Design: Cast Calligraphy

Molly and Bobby wanted an organic bohemian black tie wedding with neutral tones and pops of gold. This invitation was designed by Cast Calligraphy, and letterpress printed on 110# Cotton paper by Birdwalk Press in an unobtrusive ink sealed with a custom wax seal. Envelope calligraphy was done in a matching gold ink for a beautiful and classic aesthetic.

Amanda & Bryson's Calligraphy Invite

Design: *The Wells Makery*
Photography: *Brumley and Wells*

To the designer, there is something very romantic about calligraphy that has room to breathe and speak for itself. She focused on creating beautiful lettering and created invitations that looked great when paired with the details that A Vintage Affair Events provided and captured by the lens of Brumley and Wells Photography.

Floral Design: *The European Flower Shop*

Matahb & Masuk's
Lapidaire Suite

Design: The Wells Makery
Photography: Brumley and Wells

The inspiration for this suite was the lapidaire, or stone cutter. The team wanted to create something that had strong lines and tended towards the emotional side of romance. The shoot was taken near where the ocean roared up over the stones at Big Sur. The stationery designer used brushed calligraphy and loose watercolor mixed with straight lines and clean shapes.

Big Sky Invitation

Design: Cast Calligraphy

The Big Sky wedding invitation is one of the themes from Cast Calligraphy which is perfect for winter or summer weddings. It's a classic theme for a mountain wedding with a touch of rustic. This suite was letterpress printed in black ink on 110# Cotton Pearl White paper. Envelope calligraphy is white ink on a gravel grey envelope.

~ 155 ~

Minyi & Brian's Invitation with
Bulldog Illustration

Design: And Here We Are
Photography: And Here We Are, Levi Stolove

Minyi and Brian had a fall Brooklyn wedding in the Prospect Park Boathouse. The wedding style was classic romance with a modern and fun twist, so the team mixed a loose hand lettered script with watercolor backgrounds and chevron patterns, and also made a fun illustration of their French bulldog, Thor, for the RSVP postcards. Their colors were deep purple and succulent green, and Minyi loves all things sparkly, so metallic gold was a must. The save-the-dates and invitations feature hand-drawn letters and illustrations, which were then hand painted,

letterpress printed, and hot foil-stamped. They also included an after-party invitation on gold paper, and a tri-fold map of Brooklyn with some of Minyi and Brian's favorite Brooklyn places listed. The team printed a double run of the maps so that they could also be tucked into the welcome bags for out-of-town guests. Loads of day-of goods including menus, programs, seating chart, signage, and place cards were also created. While most of them were digitally printed, the signs were hand painted with watercolor and gold leaf gilding.

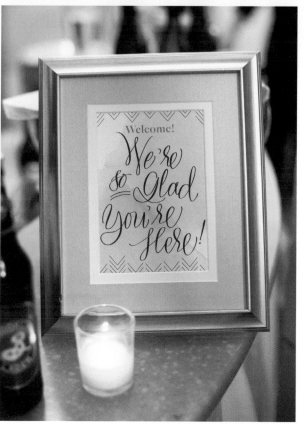

The invitation reads:

TOGETHER WITH THEIR FAMILIES

Audrey Christensen

&

John Manganaro

INVITE YOU TO JOIN THEM
ON THEIR WEDDING DAY

SATURDAY, AUGUST TWENTY-NINTH
TWO THOUSAND FIFTEEN
AT FIVE O'CLOCK IN THE AFTERNOON

ASILOMAR
800 ASILOMAR AVENUE
PACIFIC GROVE, CALIFORNIA

JOHNANDAUDREY.COM

Audrey & John's Craftsman Poppy Suite

Design: Yonder Design
Photography: Josh Gruetzmacher

This craftsman inspired suite was designed with a nod to the couple's wedding venue on the Carmel Peninsula in California, the Asilomar Center, which was designed by Julia Morgan and is one of the greatest examples of The Craftsman School of Architecture in the United States. This 3-color letterpress printed design balanced geometric patterns with a laser engraved wooden illustration of the California State Flower, the poppy.

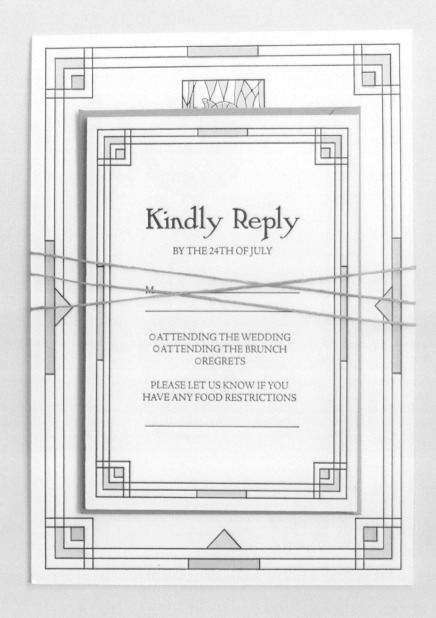

Kindly Reply

BY THE 24TH OF JULY

M

○ ATTENDING THE WEDDING
○ ATTENDING THE BRUNCH
○ REGRETS

PLEASE LET US KNOW IF YOU
HAVE ANY FOOD RESTRICTIONS

Amy & Brian's
Equestrian Wood Suite

Design: Yonder Design
Photography: Josh Gruetzmacher

This equestrian themed suite for a wedding in the mountains of Colorado was based around a custom illustration that incorporated the couple's initials. The save-the-date was laser engraved onto wood to highlight the rustic barn setting of the event. The invitation featured a patterned ribbon and custom wax closure with the couple's illustrated monogram.

KINDLY REPLY
BY
MAY 15TH

M.

○ ATTENDING
○ REGRETS

DATE OF ARRIVAL

HOTEL

TOGETHER
WITH THEIR FAMILIES

AMY KLEIN
&

...ON OF THEIR WEDDING

...HE TWENTY SECOND OF JUNE
...HOUSAND AND FOURTEEN
...O'CLOCK IN THE EVENING

...ELD BOTANICAL GARDENS
...DENVER, COLORADO

...IVITIES WILL CONTINUE
...WE DINE AND DANCE
...THE NIGHT AWAY

SAVE THE DATE
JUNE 22, 2014

FOR THE MARRIAGE OF

AMY & BRIAN

CHATFIELD BOTANICAL GARDENS
DENVER, COLORADO

FORMAL INVITATION TO FOLLOW
WWW.AMYBRIAN2014.COM

PLEASE VISIT

WWW.AMYBRIAN2014.COM

FOR ACCOMMODATIONS AND DETAILS

PLEASE JOIN US
FOR A REHEARSAL DINNER
IN HONOR OF

AMY & BRIAN

SATURDAY, JUNE 21, 2014
AT 7:00 PM

THE VILLAGE CLUB
ENGLEWOOD, COLORADO

Julie & Chris's
Joie De Vivre Suite

Design: Yonder Design
Photography: Josh Gruetzmacher

Created for a spring wedding in Provence, this suite featured a soft color palette
and French architectural rosettes. The save-the-date was printed on a silk scarf
and housed within a cylindrical walnut box. The invitations were mounted
to boards wrapped in Belgian linen affixed with brass plates reading "Joie
de Vivre." The invitations were held together within custom asymmetrical
leather clutches that guests were encouraged to keep.

NON
TOASTING FROM AFAR

M_____

KINDLY REPLY BY _____

OUI!
WE WILL BE THERE

M_____

○ Welcome Aperitif
○ Rehearsal Dinner
○ Wedding & Reception
○ Provençal BBQ

Arrival and Departure Date
in L'Isle Sur la Sorgue

_____

Kindly Reply by April 1st

SAVE THE DATE
FOR THE MARRIAGE OF

JULIE FORSBERG &
CHRIS NEUBAUER

MAY 14TH, 2015
L'ISLE SUR LA SORGUE, FRANCE

JULIECHRIS2015.COM

JOIE DE VIVRE

Amy & Adam's
Suite with Forest Moss

Design: Yonder Design
Photography: Josh Gruetzmacher

Modern typefaces and neon colors were juxtaposed with natural elements to create this one-of-a-kind suite. The screen-printed cork save-the-date arrived within a white lacquered box, filled with forest moss. The invitation featured laser etched acrylic, neon splatter paint, torn edged linen, gold foil stamping, and cork-backed paper.

**AMY &
ADAM**

WE ARE SO THRILLED THAT YOU ARE ABLE TO JOIN US
FOR THIS INCREDIBLE WEEKEND! WE ARE HUMBLED
THAT YOU HAVE TAKEN TIME OUT OF YOUR BUSY
LIVES TO CELEBRATE THE MOST IMPORTANT DAY OF
OURS. PLEASE ENJOY A FEW SNACKS AND LIBATION
ON US TO KICK OFF THE WEEKEND'S FESTIVITIES
AND GET THIS PARTY STARTED!

WE'VE PUT TOGETHER A LIST OF SOME OF OUR
FAVORITE THINGS TO DO AROUND HERE, IF YOU
NEED SOME SUGGESTIONS TO FILL OUT THE
REST OF YOUR WEEKEND.

WE CAN'T WAIT TO CELEBRATE WITH YOU!

XOXO,

AMY AND ADAM

**AMY &
ADAM**

SATURDAY, JULY 13, 2013
WOODSIDE, CALIFORNIA

FAMILY
OFFICIATED BY
DAVID DORNBUSCH

PARENTS OF THE BRIDE
MICHAEL & CAROLE MARKS

PARENTS OF THE GROOM
DAVID & HELEN DORNBUSCH

ATTENDEES
MAIDS OF HONOR
SARAH CANNON
CARLY BURTON

BEST MAN
DANIEL DORNBUSCH

BRIDESMAIDS
HEATHER MORSE
RACHEL FOX
LAURA DEBEVEC

GROOMSMEN
JUSTIN MARKS
BEN NOMURA-WEINGROW
SLOANE KRUEKLAND
BARRY CHANDLER WILLIAMS

RING BEARER
ALEX DAVID DORNBUSCH

FLOWER GIRL
OLIVIA FAITH MARKS

MUSIC PERFORMED BY
PETER DUGAN
CHARLES YANG

AMY & ADAM
6300 ACACIA AVENUE
OAKLAND, CALIFORNIA 94618

**KINDLY
RESPOND**

BY JUNE 1, 2013

M _____

WOULDN'T MISS IT FOR THE WORLD:
___ FRIDAY WELCOME PARTY
___ SATURDAY WEDDING AND RECEPTION
___ SUNDAY POST CELEBRATION BRUNCH

___ REGRETFULLY, RESPONDING FROM AFAR

Kate & Justin's
Pressed Oak Suite

Design: Yonder Design
Photography: Sylvie Gil

A muted color palette of greys, greens, and browns set the tone for this casually elegant event in Napa Valley. The pressed oak leaves were inspired by those on the property at the wedding venue. The programs were beautifully displayed on a sterling silver platter while artichokes functioned as holders for the table numbers.

Avery & Max's Modern Painting Suite

Design: Yonder Design
Photography: Josh Gruetzmacher

This modern suite sandwiched a letterpress printed card between two sheets of clear acrylic. The bottom sheet was hand brushed with thick paint to create a texture of a fine oil painting. The piece was mailed inside a clear vellum envelope with the couples logo carried throughout.

THE PARTY BEGINS

ON FRIDAY, THE TENTH OF JUNE
TWO THOUSAND SIXTEEN
AT SEVEN O'CLOCK IN THE EVENING

BAR AGRICOLE
SAN FRANCISCO, CALIFORNIA

SMART CASUAL

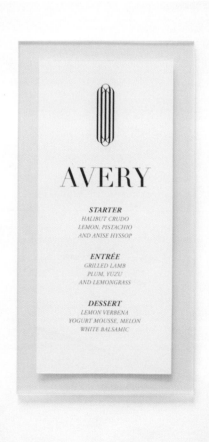

AVERY

STARTER
HALIBUT CRUDO
LEMON, PISTACHIO
AND ANISE HYSSOP

ENTRÉE
GRILLED LAMB
PLUM, YUZU
AND LEMONGRASS

DESSERT
LEMON VERBENA
YOGURT MOUSSE, MELON
WHITE BALSAMIC

YES/NO

M. _____

___ ATTENDING WE
___ ATTENDING TH
___ WISH WE COUL

KINDLY REPLY BY M

AVERY & M
2712 Pacific Avenue
San Francisco, California 94

Aldine & Ned's Suite with a Fan

Design: Mayra Monobe

The overall style of the invitation was simple yet elegant. Because the ceremony was held in a small town in Brazil, a booklet with maps, hotels, and travel information was designed to help the guests know the town better. A fan was included in the suite for the guests as a souvenir.

Liz & Nick's Wedding Guide

Design: Julia Jacqueline Warnock

As there are plenty of events on the wedding day, the team created wedding guides for guests so that they could always have something to refer to. The project consisted of customized envelopes, foldout wedding guides with bespoke die-cut and scoring, personalized foiled invitations, copper foiled stickers, maps, postcards, wedding programmes, a seating chart custom-designed on wine barrels, and all the usual "on-the-day" stationery (name cards, menus, and table numbers).

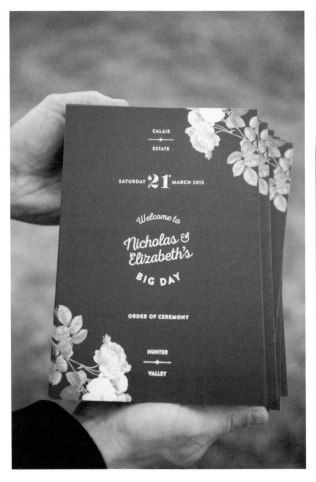

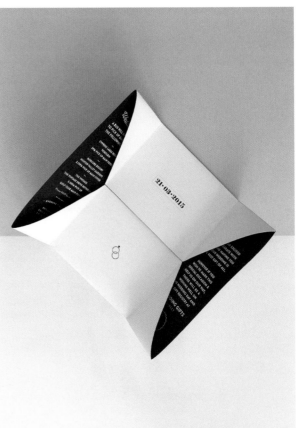

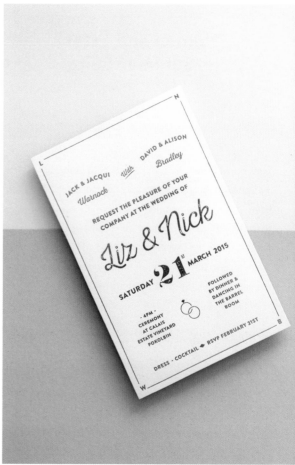

Simon and Ester's Summer Suite

Design: Ericson Corpuz

Simon and Ester's wedding was held in Horgen, Switzerland in summer, and the invitation was designed to have summer's colors and tones. The lace band went along with the Filipiniana theme of the bride and the bridesmaid's gowns, while the twine was symbolic of tying the knot. The designer also infused two mountains into the logo as one of the couple's hobbies was climbing mountains.

Eric & Arlyn's
Rustic Suite

Design: Ericson Corpuz

This project was made for the designer's own wedding. He wanted to have a very personalized invite with their own brand and monogram that would be used throughout their lives as husband and wife. The idea was to have a very earthy and rustic theme as their union was set at a quaint boutique hotel at the ridge of Tagaytay, overlooking the Taal Lake and the Taal Volcano, Philippines.

Kevin & Stephanie's Alpine Elopement Suite

Design: The Wells Makery
Photography: Brumley and Wells

Illustrations makes the invitation feel friendly, festive, and totally custom. The map in this invitation can be torn off to become a postcard, which isn't obscured by the wedding information and can be kept as a souvenir.

Jake & Annie's Rural Wedding

Stationery Design: The Wells Makery
Photography: Brumley and Wells

The bride, Annie, was the designer for the paper goods for this project, while the groom, Jack, was the photographer. After spending some time visiting Annie's family in rural Northern Colorado, the couple was inspired by the landscape up there. The high desert has a beautiful balance of rugged and elegant elements. They used sage, juniper, succulents, and rocks they found laying around the land to create this project simply for fun. The paper products are delicate but still very loose and organic, just like the sage they used to photograph them with.

Emily & Angelo's
Watercolor Invitation

Design: Sarah Drake
Photography: Julia Franzosa

Sarah painted a custom laurel wreath, banner, and other details for the save-the-date and wedding invitation for a spring wedding held at the local cultural center. The team collaborated with the calligrapher to create the mix of hand script and printed type, and digitally printed the guests' addresses in a font to coordinate. Three vintage postcards were used to give the couple options when mailing, and a watercolored band inscribed with a favorite quote held the suite together.

Calligraphy: Jilly Ink

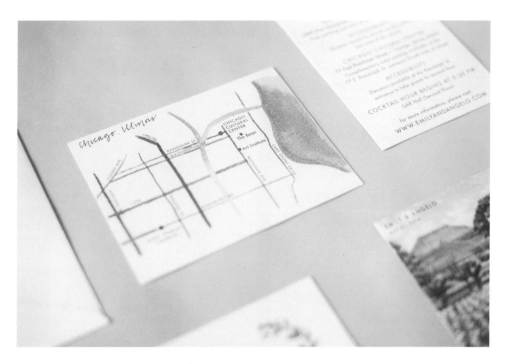

Fabio & Marina's Botanical Table Cards

Design: Mondo • Mombo
Photography: LATO Photography

Flowers were hand-painted in watercolor for these table cards. Recycled paper and a tridimensional tableau made out of cases of wine were used to create a rustic atmosphere.

Event design: Le Jour du Oui
Floral Design: Il Profumo Dei Fiori

Haslow & Ashea's
Cranberry Copper Suite

Design: Coral Pheasant Stationery
Photography: Charlotte Jenks Lewis

The stationery suite contains a mix of contrasting colors and textures. The invitation is laser etched on cognac colored leather, while the enclosure cards are accented with copper leaf detailing and the outer envelope and liner feature rich berry tones. The invitation itself is completely typeset in a script full of romantic flourishes, set at a slight angle, and is letterpress printed on double-thick Crane's Lettra. While the language on the invitation is traditional, playful wording was used on the response card.

Nora & Philipp's
60s Fusion Jazz Invitation

Design: Christian Vögtlin (ADDA Studio)

As a tribute to the couple's love of jazz, the team created invitations, name plates, menus, and thank you messages with a style evocative of 1960s fusion jazz. The rough honesty of the gray paper, which was printed black and embossed with golden hot foil, gives a playful contrast to the romantic touch of the mint green Gmund paper.

Ana & Diego's
Organic Invitation

Design: Gabriela dos Santos Biscáro

The designer created this invitation as a wedding gift for her sister. She designed organic and fluid illustrations of flowers to create something different from standard wedding iconography. The illustrations were letterpress printed, while the rest of the finishes, including the envelope, were done manually.

Emily and Dan's Green Wedding Suite

Design: A Day In May
Photography: Laura Murray Photography

Emily and Dan selected the top of Aspen Mountain to celebrate their wedding. Guest experience and comfort was a top priority and the team took great care to ensure their guests received amazing attention from start to finish. The designer chose green for the invitation suite and the name cards to bring a touch of nature and life to the guests and ceremony.

Floral Design: Carolyn's Flowers

Hiroki & Risako's Hawaiian Breeze Suite

Design: Hironobu Jyounai
(In The Castle Design Office)

Invitation using a waxed envelope and skeleton leaf pattern reminiscent of a Hawaiian breeze.

Lauren & Andrew's Cold Spring Wedding Invitation

Design: Erin Zingré

Knowing that the wedding was going to take place in Cold Spring, New York, the designer wanted the locale to inform the design. Inspired by the surrounding fall foliage, she illustrated a rustic floral pattern to off-set the ornate decorative elements of the invitation. Cold Spring is a historic town, which she wanted to reflect in the type treatments, decorative elements, and map styling. The form factor is a tri-fold panel that allows the viewer to sift through all of the event details without being overwhelmed by the information.

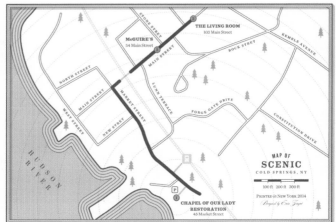

Martyna & Jacek's Natural Suite

Design: Jacek Kłosiński

The couple shares a common love for minimalism and simplicity and didn't want to make their wedding fancy or overly-glamorous. Their main goal was to make their guests feel comfortable and as at-home as possible. They used natural paper, wildflowers, and friendly texts on whole materials to create a simple, elegant, and natural style.

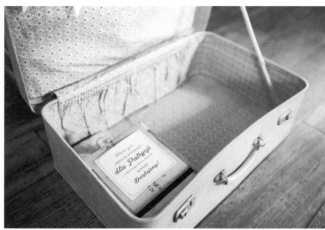

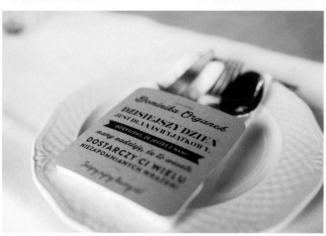

Kai & Tuan's
Folding Invitation

Design: Ray Yen (Studio Moho)
Photography: Su Lan Yu

The designer used a traditional Chinese character representing "double happiness" and a cross symbol (the couple was Christian) to create the wedding identity. The way the letter was folded imitated notes passed between school kids, implying that the couple met as children.

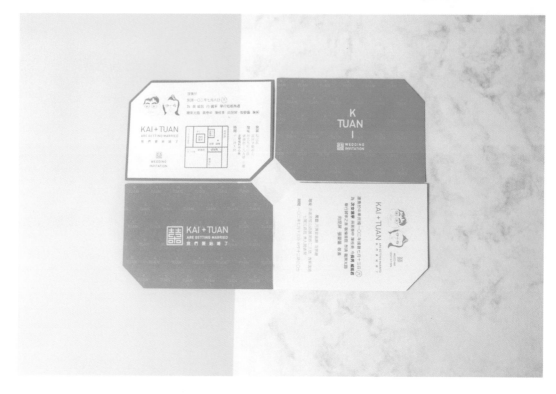

Karl & Vale's
Literary Suite

Design: Mondo • Mombo
Photography: Infraordinario Photography

Piles of antique books shape a tridimensional tableau with a vintage feel. Custom made illustrations with fresh colors and floral images modernize the whole suite.

E REGALACI *un pensiero,* DACCI *un consiglio,* DISEGNA, SCRIVICI *un messaggio,* RACCONTACI *una storia...*

Ulisse

...SÌ
E IL SUO CUORE
BATTEVA
COME IMPAZZITO
E SÌ DISSI
SÌ VOGLIO
SÌ.

James Joyce

SI STA FACENDO
sempre più
— TARDI —

IL SANGUE NON È
FATTO SOLO
DI GLOBULI BIANCHI
E ROSSI.
MA È COMPOSTO
SOPRATTUTTO
DI RICORDI.

Antonio Tabucchi

—Canti—
ORFICI

ERA INTANTO
CALATO
IL TRAMONTO
ED AVVOLGEVA
DEL SUO ORO
IL LUOGO
COMMOSSO
DAI RICORDI
E PAREVA
CONSACRARLO.

Dino Campana

Gargantua
E
Pantagruele

SE LA CARTA
DELLE MIE CAMBIALI
BEVESSE COSÌ BENE
COME ME.
I MIEI CREDITORI SI
TROVEREBBERO
A SECCO
NEL MOMENTO
DI RISCUOTERLE.

François Rabelais

Kafka
— SULLA —
SPIAGGIA

FINO A CHE
NON VERRÀ
LA MATTINA DI LUNEDÌ.
SIETE L'UNO
NELLE BRACCIA
DELL'ALTRA.
AD ASCOLTARE
IL RUMORE DEL TEMPO
CHE PASSA.

Murakami Haruki

Se una notte
D'INVERNO
UN VIAGGIATORE

ALLONTANA DA TE
OGNI ALTRO
PENSIERO.

LASCIA CHE
IL MONDO
CHE TI CIRCONDA
SFUMI
NELL'INDISTINTO

Italo Calvino

Laura and Jorge's Invitation with Symbols

Design: Santiago Amaya (Infame Studio)
Photography: Fernando Roa

Laura and Jorge's wedding invitation features the symbols of their love story: the coffee stain refers to when they met in a coffee shop in Bogotá; the clock embodies the passing of time and the winter solstice when they got together; the quill pen is a reference to when Jorge went away to study and they sadly had to be separated; the compass represents the trips they've taken together; and the flowers symbolize the love they have for each other.

Art Director: Nidia Donado

~~~~~~~~~~~~~~~~~~~~~~~~~

Jean & Wyatt's
Backyard Wedding Invitation

Design: Jolly Edition
Photography: Audra Wrisley

Wedding stationery is one of the best ways to set the scene for the wedding day, and in this case, the stunning hand-drawn illustrated stationery suite by Jolly Edition was the perfect way to introduce Jean and Wyatt's backyard wedding. The couple chose the bride's lush green backyard as their ceremony site, and styled the wedding with blush, peach, and mint accents throughout their florals and decor.

Jean Bernadette Hilpert
James Wyatt Cready Pyle

together with their parents, invite you to share the beginning
of their new life together when they exchange marriage vows

on Sunday, the sixth of
SEPTEMBER
two-thousand fifteen
at noon

in Jean's Backyard
83 Noblestown Rd
CARNEGIE, PA
15106

Ceremony
JEAN'S BACKYARD
@ 12:00PM

83 Noblestown Rd
CARNEGIE PA 15106

Luncheon
AT MONT RESTAURANT
@ 2:00PM

1114 Grandview Ave.
PITTSBURGH PA 15211

Reception
1000 GRANDVIEW PARTY ROOM
@ 6:00PM

1000 Grandview Ave.
PITTSBURGH PA 15211

Recommended Hotel for out of town guests

DOUBLETREE BY HILTON PITTSBURGH/GREENTREE
500 MANSFIELD AVE. PITTSBURGH, PA, 15205
412-922-8400

Please Visit our wedding website to RSVP by June 30th 2015
JeanAndWyatt.com password: JBN+JWCP

SAVE THE DATE

Jean Bernadette Hilpert
and
James Wyatt Cready-Pyle
September 6, 2015

Margaret & Gregory's Vintage Suite

Design: Old City Press
Photography: Audra Wrisley

These images were captured at a classic black tie wedding in Virginia, and executed and assembled by the bride herself. Designed with a blue toile pattern and vintage gold accents, this look radiates an effortless elegance reminiscent of a time long ago. Everything from the letterpress stationery to the bride's jewelry is a seamless blend of graceful style and color. The photography team documented the stationery on a gold/white fabric background, and included vintage stamps to add variety and enhance the overall aesthetic.

Chao & Xin's Invitation with Chinese Seal

Design: Wang Shi Chao

This wedding invitation was inspired by the art of Chinese seal. The designer included the names of the couple, Chao and Xin, in the seal, creating a heavily visual design with Asian sophistication and modernity.

Kohei & Natsuki's Cat-lover Invitation

Design: Hironobu Jyounai
(In The Castle Design Office)

Invitation using letterpress, gold foil, and
custom die cutting, featuring cute cat
illustrations.

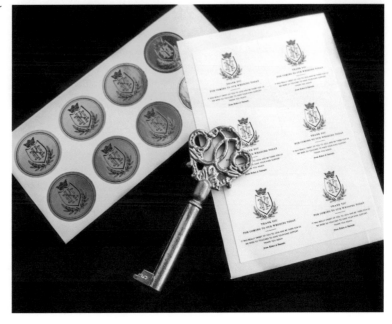

Tânia & Luís's
Invitation with Chocolate

Design: Helena Soares & Sara Costa

Inspired by the famous golden ticket of "Charlie and the Chocolate Factory," this wedding invitation was contained in a silkscreen printed box with a handmade chocolate square with the monogram relief of the couple and a golden ticket. In that way, each person invited to the wedding received a box of chocolates and was awarded with a golden ticket. The hotel Fábrica do Chocolate (Viana do Castelo, Portugal) helped the team to make 100 handmade pieces.

Marie & Nicolas's Chic Invitation

Design: Nathalie Ouederni

The designer created this wedding invitation for her best friend who wanted
something modern, chic, handmade, a little bohemian, but not too girly. The
bride loved the floral and botanical patterns the designer usually creates, so
Nathalie started from there. She made a pattern using wildflowers she hand-
drew herself, then screen-printed them in white ink with handwritten text on
gorgeous turquoise paper for the invitation. The result was a fresh and original
design with only one color printing.

Shauna & Darrell's
Tea Towel Invitation

Design: Shauna Hartsook

Shauna designed a wedding suite unlike anything else. Using a flat-bed printer, she printed the invitation on 100% cotton tea towels. The RSVP was laser etched and cut on sheets of 2mm oak. Each one is completely one-of-a-kind because of the grain of the wood. The designer also attached magnets to the back so that people could hang them on their fridge as decorations.

Jun & Yuki's
Invitation with Confetti

Design: Keiichiro Oda (AMBER)

The designer created the invitation for his handcraft artist friend whose request for the work was something amusing and casual, yet still refined. To meet that request and reflect her occupation, the team wrapped various shaped colorful confetti and an authentic invitation card together in the paper. The paper's transparency made the recipients excited even before opening it.

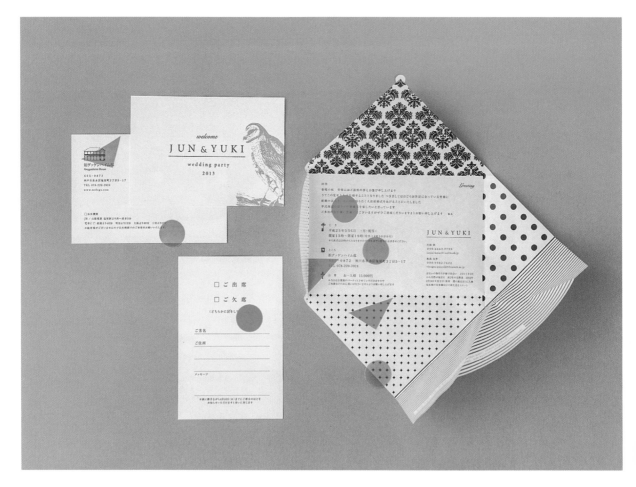

Chris & Leesa's Great Adventure

✿

Design: The Hungry Workshop

Working closely with the couple, the team decided on a theme for the wedding: it was set to be their next "Great Adventure." The wedding was a small and personal affair set in cabins amongst the bushland in the mountains of the Gold Coast Hinterland with just twenty invitations going out to close friends and family. As a result the team was able to focus their attention on craft and detail. The invitation was letterpress printed in a hand-mixed red ink on Pearl White Crane Lettra 300gsm and tucked inside a rustic envelope with a kraft string and button closure. A custom designed and embroidered merit badge with overlock-stitched edging was carefully sewn onto each invitation by hand and served as a sweet memento for the guests who took part in the "Great Adventure."

Luca & Giulia's Winter Suite

Design: Mondo • Mombo
Photography: Infraordinario Photography

White and grey paper stocks with elaborate textures were created for this winter-themed wedding. The engraving technique allows drawings and texts to appear in a play of light and shadow.

Event Design: Varese Wedding
Floral Design: Il Profumo Dei Fiori

Lucia & Igor's
Hand-colored Invitation

Design: Jan Baca

The designer avoided traditional printing and finishing methods for this project. He used a hand-colored paper with an uneven texture and had all texts written by a cutting plotter machine which had a gel pen mounted instead of knife. All invitations and menu cards had a custom monogram handwritten on the other side. The result inculded 30 sets of one-of-a-kind announcements, menu cards, and name tags.

Sarah & Asher's
Rose Gold Wedding

Stationery Design: Luminous Lines
Photography: Sposto Photography

Rose gold never goes out of style. It's elegant, feminine, and completely timeless. Featuring stunning imagery by Sposto Photography on The Loft on Pine's lower level, this shoot was styled with some of Los Angeles and Orange County's finest wedding vendors.

Event Design: Green Apple Event
Floral Design: Little Hill Floral Design
Backdrop Design: Drop It Modern

Nadia & Chad's French Provincial Invitation

Design: The Hungry Workshop

To escape the hustle and bustle of San Diego, the couple travelled all the way to the small French provincial town of Eygalières via Paris with their closest friends and family to celebrate their wedding. Since the destination is obviously the exclamation point of any journey, creating an invitation that was also a map seemed particularly fitting. Letterpress printed in a metallic gold ink over a soft pink map of France, the invitation laid out the adventure before the guests with carefully crafted art nouveau typography. A short reading list and a few handy phrases were included on the invitation, all tucked into custom string and button envelopes. The large format of the invitation required the team to print the maps on their Asbern Proof Press. Each sheet was hand fed twice through the press and then folded to fit into the envelopes.

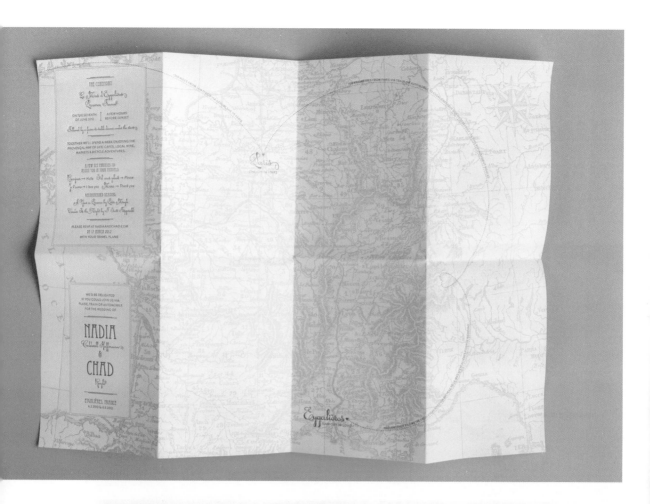

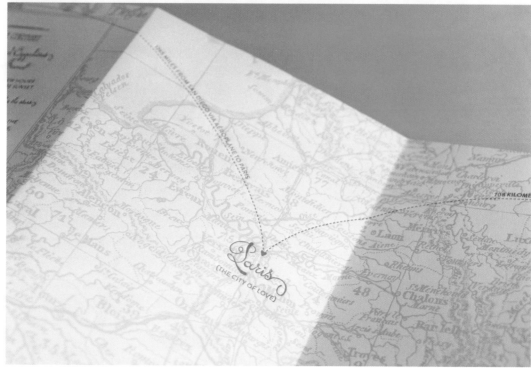

Christina & Aaron's Invitation with Playful Wording

Design: Patti Murphy
Photography: Ania Simpson,
Michelle Gardella Photography

Christina and Aaron wanted their wedding invitations to reflect their personalities through vibrant colors and playful wording. Shades of orange and teal were their wedding colors, so these colors were incorporated along with a favorite quote often attributed to Dr. Seuss. The invitation suite is both whimsical and varied, to further display the playfulness of their personalities. In addition to the lively fonts and colors, Christina and Aaron wanted to incorporate letterpress chipboard, as well as custom stamps to give the invites a more handcrafted look. The invites, an accordion-folded booklet, and RSVP postcards were all stacked together and tied with twine.

Event Design: Ambiance Luxe Wedding Design
Letterpress Printing: Kismet Letterpress

Amanda & Brandan's
Ibiza Suite

Design: Mondo • Mombo
Photography: Ana Lui Photography

For this wedding stationery made with acrylic painting and collage,
a boho style was accomplished through geometric forms and
textures, which are evocative of colorful Persian rugs.

Event Design: Le Jour du Oui
Floral Design: Flowers Ibiza

Wedding Graphic
Elements

Fonts: Dancing Script OT, BlackJack, Bebas Neue

SAVE
THE
DATE

PAUL & EMMA

THE

Thank You Love

THANK YOU

INVITATION

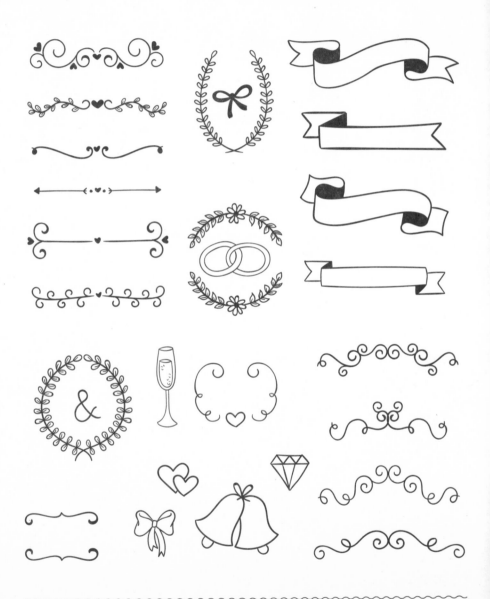

ORNAMENTS

YOUR TEXT
JUST HERE

OUR

the

and

wedding

from

with

Mr. & Mrs.

Wedding Ornament

SAVE THE DATE

Fonts: BlackJack, Euphoria Script

Fonts: BlackJack, Euphoria Script, Kaushan Script, Nexa

Save the Date

Mr & Mrs

Save the Date

&

love love

Wedding

love love

&

&

&

Save the Date

Yes, I do!!

Save the Date

Fonts: Raleway, Rochester

Fonts: Abril Fatface, OSP DIN

• Index •

Index

Index

techniques, she runs a small creative studio working on printed products, branding small businesses, and custom projects. Passionate in conceptual projects and visual storytelling, inspired by urban culture and nature, she gives all her designs a personal touch.

Ericson Corpuz
www.ericsonrcorpuz.weebly.com

As a photographer, Eric is good at visual storytelling and capturing fleeting moments with an innate eye for creativity. Graduated in journalism at the University of the Philippines, his knowledge lends drama and artistry to his works including portraiture, travel, landscape, photojournalism, architecture, fashion, events, and documentary.

Erin Zingré
www.erinzingre.com

Graduated in visual communication and art history from the University of Kansas, starting her career at Tractorbeam in Dallas, where she worked on several branding projects, award-winning graphic designer and illustrator Erin currently works as a visual designer at Amazon in Seattle. In her spare time, she works on a self-published zine Beasts of Fancy cataloging various mythological creatures. She has also illustrated for a coloring book.

FØLSOM Studio
www.folsom-studio.fr

A Paris-based multidisciplinary creative studio, whose name means delicate and meticulous in Norwegian and serves as

the guideline of the team. It is composed of three designers who enjoy appeasing their clients by adapting to their needs and ambitions. They work on stage, graphic, interior, and product design as a collective, sharing their skills to conceive complete and coherent concepts.

Gabriela dos Santos Biscáro
www.behance.net/gabiscaro

A self-taught Sao Paulo-based illustrator and graphic designer with 5 years expereince focused on editorial illustration and branding. She enjoys painting and making things manually. Plans to work for children's books in the future and bring more color to more people's lives.

Giorgia Smiraglia
www.giorgiasmiraglia.com

Inspired by illustration, typography, and fine arts, with good design sensitivity and great attention to detail, graphic designer Giorgia loves clean execution, has firm respect for rigour, and considers conceptual thinking fundamental to the success of any project.

GRAPHO_MAT
www.behance.net/GRAPHOMAT

Created by graphic designer Andreea Mihaiu, textile designer Mihai Popescu, and product designer Andra Pavel, all graduates of the National University of Arts, Bucharest, GRAPHO_MAT explores the process behind every project, and works at the intersection of multiple fields including graphic design, branding, textile design, manual bookbinding, product design, and illustration.

Helena Soares & Sara Costa
www.behance.net/helenacmorais-s
www.behance.net/saramoreirac

Two Portugueese designers with simillar backgrounds. Helena graduated in communication design at the Faculty of Fine Arts, University of Porto, currently attends the master of communication design program at ESAD, Escola Superior de Artes e Design, and works as a freelancer designer/illustrator with many international publications. Sara also graduated in communication design but at ESAD, and recently works as a freelance illustrator.

Hironobu Jyounai
www.dj-jyounai.net

A Tokyo-based DJ, producer, and art director who considers himself a "very very happening cat."

Infame Studio
www.infamestudio.com

A design studio that aims to transcend mere ideas, and to communicate and create experiences through careful and detailed work.

Jacek Kłosiński
www.klosinski.net

A Gdansk-based graphic designer and blogger who likes to help creative people.

Jan Baca
www.janbaca.net

Graduated in graphic and product design, Slovak multidisciplinary

Index

designer Jan had worked at several design firms before he started his freelance career in 2015 specializing in packaging design and branding for global clients. Jan's work has been featured regularly on prestigious blogs focused on packaging design and other design publications.

Joel Serrato
www.joelserrato.com

Life and happenstance led Joel to become a filmmaker and photographer who infuses his love of movement in capturing moments of innocence, laughter, love, and life. He has carved out a niche in the filmmaking world as the reigning king of Super 8 weddings, taking the art of storytelling to a whole new level. His films are pure emotion wrapped in the artistic coupling of nostalgic moments with intimate takes on real life.

Jon Jackson
www.cargocollective.com/lagraphica

Designer with 20 years experience, currently a partner at Brooklyn-based studio Work & Company, where he leads design across products and brand-focused engagements. Jon has created integrated brand experiences for world class clients such as Target, Acura, Nissan, Fandango, Chase Bank, and Walt Disney.

Julia Jacqueline Warnock
www.juliajacque.com

A Sydney-based multidisciplinary designer.

Kathy Ager
www.kathyager.com

Amsterdam-based graphic designer and fine artist who studied graphic design and illustration at Capilano University in Vancouver, Canada, and started her career at DDB Vancouver before relocating to Europe. She founded her own design studio in 2012 aiming to bring clients' messages to life in unique and visually impactful ways, and has served both large and small, local and international clients since its inception.

Keiichiro Oda
www.amber-d.net

Art director and president of design studio AMBER, whose motto is "conveying feelings as well as information" and "transparency," with a simple and clear design style. Always adding some elements to make the heart beat faster, AMBER helps its clients to communicate with their audience.

Kelsy Stromski
www.refinery43.com

Designer, creative director, and brand stylist who founded Refinery 43 and loves adventure, food, and beautiful typography.

Lara Hotz Photography
www.larahotz.com

A studio that believes photography is a way of telling stories, capturing moments, and finding beauty in unlikely places at its best when underscored by truth.

Laura Murray Photography
www.lauramurrayphotography.com

Laura is a wedding and portrait photographer based out of Denver, Colorado. She was trained in mathematics prior to photography but has always had a desire for creativity in her life. There were always two sides to her – a technical and a creative. Luckily she found photography which is the perfect blend of both. Laura and her husband spend their free time traveling the world as much as they can, always looking for new adventures. They also enjoy keeping active in their beautiful state with hiking, cycling, and snow-shoeing. Photography is most certainly Laura's passion manifested into a dream job.

MaeMae & Co.
www.maemaeco.com

A creative studio and nationally recognized wedding stationery brand founded by Megan Gonzalez, who genuinely connects to an audience by sharing inspiring stories about her creative process and creating compelling product imagery. Passionate about coming alongside other entrepreneurs and creative teams to assist them in telling their story, Megan currently works as an art director, stylist, and, designer.

Mayra Monobe
www.mayramonobe.com

Born in São Paulo, Japanese-Brazilian graphic designer and illustrator Mayra graduated from The Billy Blue School of Design and Elisava School of Design and Engineering (with a master degree). Collaborating with companies like

Index

Hulsbosch Communications and The Creative Method in Australia and Talking Design, Eumogràfic, Clase Bcn in Barcelona, she has been recognized by ADG-FAD, Pentawards, Graphis, AGDA, Create Awards, among others.

Mondo • Mombo
www.mondomombo.it

An Italy-based design studio.

Nathalie Ouederni
www.nathalieouederni.com

Barcelona-based French illustrator and designer who loves working with watercolors to create botanical and floral patterns, food illustrations, and nature inspired scenes, and enjoys working on custom projects like invitations, branding projects, and custom illustrations.

Nathan Parker
www.behance.net/nathanwparker

A Sweden-based graphic designer with a passion for branding and identity creation. Nathan enjoys clean and simple design with striking visual elements.

Park & Grove
www.parkandgrove.com

A Los Angeles-based full service event design and production studio created in 2013 by Sarah Tolboe and Marla Weintraub with a combined 14+ years experience in the event industry, who share an overwhelming passion for events and a meticulous eye for design more than anything.

Patti Murphy
www.pattimurphydesigns.com

A full service creative design studio based in Mystic, Connecticut, USA, specializing in branding, print, and event collateral design.

Pedro Loustau
www.photographelabaule.com

A talented photographer good at catching simple and beautiful moments with discretion and professionalism, specialized in wedding and portrait photography.

Sarah Drake
www.sarahdrakedesign.com

A Chicago-based photographer and designer who creates ready- and custom-made wedding suites and decor, personalized crests, stationery, and fine items for the home.

Sarah Kate
www.sarahkatephoto.com

A Dallas-based wedding photographer with a particular affection for people and adventure, who crafts unique stories as they are witnessed through the lens by carefully integrating people and objects within their spaces to imbue them with further beauty and meaning. She has been commissioned to shoot projects all over the world, and is available for local and international travel for wedding days and beyond.

Shauna Hartsook
www.shaunamae.ca

An award-winning art director and graphic designer based in Calgary, Alberta, Canada. Over the course of her decade-long career, Shauna has won multiple awards including a Cannes Bronze Lion, a One Show Silver Pencil Award, and multiple Ad Rodeo Anvil Awards. Shauna currently heads up the curated online store Fairgoods.com, a company that specializes in unique items that emphasize typography. She also does freelance graphic design in her spare time.

Sofia Invitations and Prints
www.sofiainvitations.com

An internationally known luxury wedding invitation and design company producing expertly crafted goods with the best materials, everlasting designs and unique techniques such as letterpress printing, laser cutting, and wood engraving. Also works with large and small businesses to create custom and luxurious printed materials including letterpress business cards and invitations for special events.

Sposto Photography
www.spostophotography.com

A wedding photography studio based in Long Beach, CA, created by Shelby and Shauntelle 10 years ago shortly after they began their relationship. The couple enjoys working together as a team with each displaying different strengths that amount to one great unit. They love connecting with their clients and everything there is to photograph at weddings.

Index

Studio Caserne
www.studiocaserne.ca

A graphic design studio developing projects with a holistic approach, rooted in utility, consistency, and relevance.

P.126-127

Studio Moho
www.studiomoho.com

A multidisciplinary creative office that serves as a visual storyteller and strategist for a wide range of local and international corporate clients, organizations, individuals, and self-initiated projects. Focused on communicating clear messages through a carefully-resolved aesthetic, its designs are based on concepts and transfer its clients' inspirations.

P.200-201

Sylvain Toulouse
www.sylvaintoulouse.com

A Montreal-based freelance art director and graphic designer who specializes in visual identity and logo design, offers a full spectrum of graphic design services both in print and digital, and makes no compromises with achieving the highest quality possible for each design project. His creative work has been published in worldwide design books, trade magazines, and notable design websites and blogs.

P.092-093

Tessa Persoons
www.behance.net/TessaPersoons

A Belgian graphic designer currently working at "Famous Advertising."

P.118-119

The Hungry Workshop
www.thehungryworkshop.com.au

Specialized in identity, packaging, stationery, web, and letterpress print projects, The Hungry Workshop was created by Simon and Jenna Hipgrave with a collective 18 years industry experience to deliver their passion for storytelling through design, process, craft, and collaboration. They often roll up their sleeves, getting their hands dirty to create a perfect execution.

P.128-129, 221, 228-229

The Pick of the Crab
www.pik.cl

A design lab dedicated to illustrations, graphics, corporate gifts, and independent publications. The fresh pick for the good design.

P.108-109

The Wells Makery
www.thewellsmakery.com

An illustration and hand lettering studio nestled in the Rocky Mountains of Southwest Colorado, run by Annie Brooks and Whitney Watts, specializing in decadent florals, custom maps and portraits, and modern calligraphy.

P.150-153, 182-183

Tom Pitts
www.tompitts.co.uk

Specialized in branding, print, and web design, Tom draws techniques from website and app design and merges them with traditional techniques like print. He has worked for world-class brands including Universal Music, Island Records, Bupa, Shell, and NHS for multidisciplinary projects.

P.090-091

Wang Shi Chao
www.behance.net/wsc-design

A graphic designer based in Taiwan.

P.212

Yonder Design
www.yonderdesign.com

Generally involved at the early stages of an event, the team specializes in conceptualizing and designing save-the-dates, websites, and invitations, assisting event planners in executing and developing their ideas to create cohesive and well branded events. Their initial graphic designs, which lay the framework of elements that will be carried through to the actual event itself, are all done in their San Francisco-based studio.

P.022-027, 130-133, 160-171

• Acknowledgements •

We would like to thank all of the designers involved for granting us permission to publish their works, as well as all of the photographers who have generously allowed us to use their images. We are also very grateful to many other people whose names do not appear in the credits but who made specific contributions and provided support. Without these people, we would not have been able to share these beautiful works with readers around the world. Our editorial team includes editor Guo Daze and book designer Wu Yanting, to whom we are truly grateful.